HISTORIC
YOSEMITE NATIONAL PARK

The Stories Behind One of America's Great Treasures

TRACY SALCEDO

Guilford, Connecticut

An imprint of Rowman & Littlefield

Distributed by NATIONAL BOOK NETWORK

British Library Cataloguing in Publication Information Available

Library of Congress Cataloging-in-Publication Data

Names: Salcedo-Chourré, Tracy, author.
Title: Historic Yosemite National Park : the stories behind one of America's
  great treasures / Tracy Salcedo.
Description: Guilford, Connecticut : Lyons Press, [2016] | Includes
  bibliographical references and index.
Identifiers: LCCN 2016003161 (print) | LCCN 2016003680 (ebook) | ISBN
  9781493018116 (pbk.) | ISBN 9781493018123 (e-book)
Subjects: LCSH: Yosemite National Park (Calif.)—History. | Yosemite National
  Park (Calif.)—Biography.
Classification: LCC F868.Y6 S193 2016 (print) | LCC F868.Y6 (ebook) | DDC
  979.4/47—dc23
LC record available at http://lccn.loc.gov/2016003161

∞™ The paper used in this publication meets the minimum requirements of American National Standard for Information Sciences—Permanence of Paper for Printed Library Materials, ANSI/ NISO Z39.48-1992.

For the TP Princesses,
who know best why "dollops of wilderness" mean so much to me

Contents

Author's Note

On the Brilliance of Faraway Eyes

I can't claim the cliché that Yosemite changed my life. My love of exploring wild places was determined long before I walked in the park.

But Yosemite helped. My first backpacking trip was a two-week tour of the park's backcountry with a Sierra Studies class from my high school in 1978. I wish now I'd paid closer attention, so I could tell you our route. I know we started in Tuolumne Meadows; I remember fumbling the word around in my mouth when I saw it on the sign. We climbed Cathedral Peak; it was my first true mountaintop, and I saw the curve of the Earth for the first time from the summit. The rest is a magical blur of walking and looking, walking and looking, day after day, until I felt as shiny and solid as the rock underfoot, and my breath felt easy no matter the slope, and the ground beneath my thin sleeping pad was actually comfortable.

That trip helped anchor a passion for walking in wilderness that has never ebbed. Not that I let anyone know at the time; I was a teenager, after all. The friends who convinced me to take the class were sure I hated it. The food was nasty. That first meal from a foil pouch I dubbed "hairy chicken and maggots," and I've never gotten over the crime that is dehydrated eggs. I won an award for the massive blisters that developed on my heels; even the kids on the bus home were aghast when I finally took off my boots in public. It takes a good amount of gross to make a teenage boy cringe.

But if anything speaks to the power of Yosemite, it's those blisters. I had to hide them from the instructors, as we'd been warned that if we got hurt, we'd be sent home, and blisters counted, since they could get infected. I didn't want to leave, so I powered through. Discovering the best way to avoid the pain was to not stop walking, I hiked from camp to camp without break. The poor teacher who had to keep tabs on me only got me to stop when he brought out the map and compass. I don't remember the names of the pass we stood on or the steep-walled valley we gazed down, but I remember it clicking: lines on paper to peaks on a ridgeline, this one with a sheer wall on the north side, this one a dome. Now I was free to wander.

I also don't remember the name of the trail we took down into Yosemite Valley, but I do remember the massive camps on the floor. This was a time when Yosemite struggled with crowds packed in campgrounds and in long lines of traffic on the loop road. Trailers were parked side by side between the trees, a subdivision complete with clotheslines and televisions with rabbit-ear antennas. As elated as I'd been on the mountaintop, I deflated among the Airstreams.

I understand now that I came out of Yosemite's backcountry with faraway eyes. I've come to know them well over the years, having seen them in friends and family, and recognizing them in myself. Faraway eyes come with time spent scanning horizons for days on end, whether on a boat or on foot or even looking out a car window on a long road trip. What has struck me, as I've worked on *Historic Yosemite National Park*, is how often I see faraway eyes in the pictures of Yosemite's heroes. Especially when they gaze past the camera, you get the impression they are looking way over, way up, beyond. In those days, I imagine, it couldn't be helped. There were no rabbit-ear TVs or cell phones to pull you in. It was all up and out.

The knowledge of faraway eyes informs all the essays in this book. To understand how Yosemite came to be what it is—the "flagship," the "crown jewel," the "mountain temple" of America's national park system— an understanding of how the place affects the people who've visited, and especially the people who've lived it, is prerequisite. You can't truly *be* in Yosemite without losing yourself in distance and time.

Of the people who lived here, I am in awe of their fortitude, their bravery, and their luck. They created homes in a wild place so monumental it's impossible not to look faraway all the time. Somehow, still, they managed to bake bread, split rails, break trails, raise crops, and keep the books for their camps and hotels. All the while the mountains embraced them, the waterfalls formed the backbeat, the meadows bloomed, and

The sun catches on clouds breaking over Sentinel Rock. PHOTO: TRACY SALCEDO

the river flowed. Drudgery amid such beauty requires a special kind of discipline.

On that first backpacking trip, having seen all that makes Yosemite superlative, I also saw the park's dark side. I'll admit, I've avoided the Valley in summertime ever since. I can't take the crowds. I can't take the noise, the push, and these days, the focus on the device over the mind's eye as the receptacle of memory. You can't experience faraway when your eyes are fixed on the screen at arm's length.

I close my eyes and I see the full moon square in the notch on Half Dome's sheer face, the rainbow at the base of Vernal Fall, the glittering slide of Staircase Falls, the heart-clenching exposure from Columbia Rock, the endless views from the top of Sentinel Dome. Even with lids shut, I can enjoy the blessings of Yosemite's first gift to me—the gift of faraway eyes.

INTRODUCTION

When we try to pick out anything by itself, we find it hitched to everything else in the universe.

—JOHN MUIR

As it turns out, there are two wildernesses in Yosemite. One is full of domes and waterfalls and deep woods; the other is composed of thousands of pages recording the park's natural and cultural history.

And just as trailblazers wound through Yosemite's vast and convoluted backcountry establishing routes so others could follow, so too have there been trailblazers among Yosemite's historians. From explorers like Lafayette Bunnell to conservationists like John Muir, from researchers like Shirley Sargent, Hank Johnston, and Carl P. Russell to the rangers who today compose blog posts for the park's Nature Notes series, they have plumbed stories, journals, newspapers, superintendents' reports, government documents, private photographic collections, and their own experiences to tell Yosemite's story. Each writer, no matter their calling or trade, has contributed valuable personal insights into the most wondrous of America's national parks.

This is a humble addition to that treasury.

History is a moving target. Just as wind and water continue to sculpt Yosemite's landscapes, mind and pen reshape its story. How the park came to be known as *Yosemite* is perhaps the best example of how fluid this can be. Different spellings—*uzamati,* Yo-Hemite, Yo-Semite—all come into play in different documents, along with different meanings. Which is right? We might never know with certainty; the original speakers and writers are long gone, and other resources may be uncovered down the line. But the search is as much a part of Yosemite's story as the truth.

One thing remains constant, threading through every book and every document about Yosemite National Park: the writer's passion for the

Half Dome PHOTO: TRACY SALCEDO

place. It's what hitches them to each other, from John Muir to Galen Clark to Shirley Sargent to the ranger leading the next interpretive hike on the Valley floor. These essays, which explore both new and well-trod terrain, in turn hitch me, and those who read what I've composed, with those who have come before. The idea is to present old stories in small bites with fresh perspective. I do not have Muir's poetic flair, but in a new age, in a new time, when the wilderness philosophy has begun to spin back toward an awareness that we are all part of a greater, grander whole, different words can be used, to similar effect.

Interpretive ranger Christine Loberg stood beside a young sequoia on the edge of Cook's Meadow, the sun filtering through scudding storm clouds and falling November leaves. Her voice filled with emotion, she described how four people had worked to save the Yosemite temple: Lincoln, through his signature on the Yosemite Grant Act; Galen Clark, as Yosemite's longtime guardian; John Muir, with his prolific pen; and Ansel Adams, with his photographs. My hope is that this little book—this Yosemite in a hundred words—will hitch itself to the traditions that led to the preservation of America's most celebrated national park.

The Ahwahneechee

JULIA PARKER WAS LATE. SHE'D PROMISED TO BE AT THE YOSEMITE Museum by nine a.m. to teach a visitor how to make a brush out of soaproot, but she'd missed her bus. When she arrived, she settled on the corner of a raised platform in the museum, surrounded by cultural artifacts: beautiful basketware behind glass; beaded clothing; arrows and spears; and the materials necessary to make all of these things. She spread her cotton skirt and apron, and pulled the root out of her bag. She'd dug it up that morning, and when she was done, she'd replant it.

Then she set to work.

Julia is an interpreter. She's also Native American. She worked in Yosemite National Park for decades before retiring in 2015 at the age of eighty-six. Her job was to tell visitors about the Ahwahneechee, the "first people" who lived in the Valley, and to show how those people made their living here.

Julia's also a master basket weaver. Her fingers, through riddled with arthritis, manifest skills that have been passed from mother to daughter through generations of the Ahwahneechee and the other Miwok tribes of California. She was born on the Graton Rancheria north of San Francisco, and married a Sierra Miwok, a distant son of the Ahwahneechee. That is her connection to Yosemite. In many ways she's a rock star: Her name resonates among students of California's Native history.

The baskets created by California's Indian women are utilityware. They used these meticulously woven vessels in all aspects of their lives: for gathering acorns and other footstuffs, for winnowing the husks and shells from acorn meats, for cooking, for carrying their children. After the "white man" came, with tools they insisted were better suited to those tasks—wooden boxes, metal screens, cast-iron pans, prams—the women, demonstrating the flexibility of the survivor, recast their baskets as souvenirs. For decades, the descendants of the Ahwahneechee continued to make baskets in Yosemite; it was a way to stay alive and in their ancestral place.

For Julia Parker, the tradition has additional meaning. She is also a teacher, helping park visitors gain some understanding of who Yosemite's Indians were, and the gifts they left on the land. Her age-twisted fingers are nimble as she meticulously fashions whatever it is she is making. She tells stories while she works. In doing these things, she honors those who came before her.

The First People

Yosemite's "first people" called themselves the Ahwahneechee after the valley they lived in: *Ahwahnee*, "place like a gaping mouth." Neighboring tribes, however, and later, the first settlers, called the Valley Natives the Yosemites, which has been translated as both "those who kill" and, perhaps erroneously, "grizzly bear." Ferocious translations for a tribe that most ethnographers describe as essentially peaceful—but a tribe that would, when confronted, fiercely defend its homeland.

Human habitation in the Yosemite Valley has been traced back to about 6000 BC. What those first people called themselves and how they were related to neighboring tribes is unknowable. But the Ahwahneechee are part of a larger California tribal group called the Miwok, which includes geographically separate subtribes located many miles distant. To understand how a band of Natives living in Yosemite could be related to a band living in the coastal valleys north of San Francisco (the Coast Miwok), a band living farther north near Clear Lake (the Lake Miwok), and other bands farther north in the Sierra Nevada, a quick primer on the variety and interconnectedness of California's precolonial makeup is in order.

Look at a map of tribal boundaries in the mid-eighteenth century, before contact and as conceptualized by modern anthropologists, and California is a stunning mosaic. The state's population numbered roughly 200,000 before the arrival of Spanish missionary, military, and exploratory expeditions in the late eighteenth century, but what's illuminating is the number of tribes that represents. Today, the federal government recognizes 109 California tribes, with another 78 petitioning for recognition. These tribes are delineated not only by location but also by linguistics, with as many as ninety different languages identified, and dialects numbering in the hundreds. It's the umbrella of a linguistic group that links the Coast Miwok of the Bay Area to the Southern Sierra Miwok of the Yosemite Valley.

To add further depth, the Ahwahneechee was not the only tribe to occupy or visit what would later become Yosemite National Park. The Mono Lake Paiute lived on the eastern slope of the Sierra, the Central Sierra Miwok lived along the Stanislaus and Tuolumne Rivers to the north, and Yokut territory was to the west. Despite the rugged terrain, these tribes were not isolated: They visited each other, made war on each other, maintained trade with each other, and intermarried.

The peak precontact population of Yosemite Valley and the park at large is unknown, but those numbers had been cut significantly by the time Yosemite Valley was "discovered" in the mid-nineteenth century. Chief Tenaya of the Yosemite Indians would tell park guardian Galen Clark of a "fatal black sickness" that, along with warfare, decimated his tribe. Though Yosemite's Indians never had direct contact with the Spanish missionaries who brought, among other things, devastating disease to tribes on Alta California's coast, those same diseases appear to have passed, tribe by tribe, to the Indians of the interior valleys and eventually into the Sierra Nevada. Chief Tenaya tallied two hundred members in his tribe in 1851, when the Mariposa Battalion campaigned to remove them.

California's Native cultural and linguistic diversity did not last. A century after first contact, disease, starvation, and warfare had depleted Native numbers in the state to an estimated twelve thousand souls. Some tribes vanished completely, notably the Yahi, whose last member, Ishi, would make headlines when he emerged from the foothills near what is now Lassen Volcanic National Park at the turn of the twentieth century. Ishi would spend the rest of his days helping anthropologists at the University of California, Berkeley, understand a way of life that had been extirpated. Ishi was alone, but he was not; other last members of lost tribes passed from California's wild places without fanfare or record. Still, some

Natives endured, among them Californians of Ahwahneechee descent, though the last surviving full-blood members of the tribe have, like Ishi, passed into history.

SPLENDID ISOLATION

Ahwahnee, in season, provided everything its people needed.

Food was plentiful in the Valley. California black oaks, sprawling trees that, prior to the mid-1800s, were cultivated by the Ahwahneechee, provided acorns, the staple grain. The Ahwahneechee used fire to keep the oaks from being crowded out by evergreens; this practice also kept the Valley floor relatively clear of brush and tinder, thus reducing the danger of raging wildfire. The nuts of the black oak were gathered in fall, stored in granaries, and prepared in a variety of ways.

Processing acorns into edible meal is time-consuming. The nuts must be ground, then leached of the tannins that make them bitter. To do this,

Maggie Howard, also known as Ta-bu-ce, prepares acorns. COURTESY OF THE YOSEMITE NATIONAL PARK ARCHIVES, MUSEUM, AND LIBRARY

the Ahwahneechee women would crack the nut, peel away and discard its hard shell, then grind the nutmeats with mortar and pestle. Mortar rocks, such as one found behind the Yosemite Museum and another located near Lower Yosemite Fall, are scattered around the Valley, round holes worn into the granite over generations. Leaching the tannins required flowing water, so the meal was placed in baskets in the Valley's streams, which carried the bitterness away. Once the meal was sweet, it was cooked in baskets as mush or baked as cakes.

Ahwahneechee women gathered other edibles in season as well, including berries and the nuts of other trees. Men provided by hunting wild game—mule deer, bear, and smaller creatures like squirrels and birds. They also fished, sometimes using the toxic properties of native plants, such as soaproot bulbs and buckeye nuts, to stun trout in a stream so they'd be easier to catch.

The materials for basket-making were plentiful. The foundation and frame of the Ahwahneechee basket is willow, which grows in thickets along the banks of the Merced River. Redbud, blooming fluorescent pink in spring, is harvested after the first frost and the first rain, "two eyes above the ground," and is the red accent found in basket designs. When bracken fern matures in the summer, part of the root stem is harvested and used for the black accents. All the materials are carefully tended and allowed to cure for a year before use; every basket takes "a season to make."

The biggest village in the Yosemite Valley was located near the base of Yosemite Falls (called *Cho-lok*). Dwellings constructed of brush or the distinctive bark of the incense cedar surrounded ceremonial structures, including a sweathouse, which was used for purification, helping hunters to rid themselves of their scent so prey would be unaware of their presence. In the roundhouse, the people gathered to pray and sing and dance. Music enlivened the gatherings, with percussion tapped out using "clapper sticks"—elderberry boughs that had been dried, split, and fashioned into an instrument that produced a hand-clap drumbeat. The remains of the Yosemite Falls village were uncovered when the Yosemite Museum and other structures in the modern Yosemite Village were built in the early 1920s. In the years since, the National Park Service and local Indians have come together to reconstruct the village as it might have been

Susie McGowan carries her baby, Sophie, in a cradle basket. PHOTO: J.T. BOYSEN, 1900. COURTESY OF THE YOSEMITE NATIONAL PARK ARCHIVES, MUSEUM, AND LIBRARY

pre-contact, including a round-house and sweathouse that are still used.

Smaller villages were scattered elsewhere in the Valley; guardian Galen Clark puts the number at eight. Spectacular sites were chosen for the satellites as well, with villages at the base of Sentinel Rock, El Capitan, and the Three Brothers. The people would come together to work and hunt, and for celebrations, feasts, and games. The valley villages were seldom occupied year-round; like other tribes in the Sierra Nevada, the Ahwahneechee would retreat to lower altitudes—in this case, down the Merced—to avoid winter's heavy snows and freezing temperatures.

What the Valley couldn't provide, the Ahwahneechee would acquire from neighbors. Obsidian for arrowheads, for example, was obtained from the Mono Paiute, who lived seventy miles to the east at Mono Lake. The Yosemite Indians may have had a reputation for fierceness, but that did not interfere with the trade that all California tribes regularly took part in.

Conservation was a way of life for the Ahwahneechee. The things they needed were harvested at the optimal time, and in such a way that the source could survive. The soaproot that Julia Parker used to make a brush is a perfect example, as the bulb would grow another brush when returned to the earth. Redbud, willow, and bracken fern were also harvested sustainably.

If preservation were not possible, every possible part of the plant or animal was used in some fashion: leaves, stem, sap, and root; meat, skin, feather, sinew, and bone. In the case of the incense cedar, the bark was used to build homes, and the heartwood, when dried out, was made into portable fire "drills": Spun into a hole on another piece of wood, the friction would create heat, then a spark.

In these ways, as interpretive ranger Phil Johnson explains, the Ahwahneechee were able to "live off the land and live with the land" for several thousand years.

The Stories They Told

The epic landforms of the Yosemite Valley inspired the Ahwahneechee in the same way they inspired those who followed. And like those who followed, Yosemite's Indians gave names to the domes, waterfalls, arches, and rivers, some of which persist on the landscape, and some now secondary to what appears on US Geological Survey maps and in park literature.

The story of Half Dome? As John Muir tells it, its origin is in glaciation. For climbers, it is a first ascent, a new route, an epic survival story. For day hikers Half Dome is epic as well, a test of endurance and the ability to tolerate exposure; a bucket-list story. For the Ahwahneechee, the story of *Tis-si-ak*, as the monolith is known, is one of family discord, and that story encompasses some of the surrounding landmarks as well.

As the story goes, Tis-si-ak, with her husband and child, were traveling into *Ahwahnee* from far away. She carried a burden basket and the baby in a basket as well. As they had traveled a long distance, Tis-si-ak was thirsty, so when she reached the clear waters of *Ah-wei-ya* (Mirror Lake), she drank it dry. Her husband was so furious he beat her; she, in turn, became enraged and berated him, throwing her burden basket at him. For their "wickedness," all were turned to stone. Tis-si-ak became what we call Half Dome; her tears streak her sheer face. Her husband, the North Dome, hunkers nearby; the burden basket became Basket Dome; and the innocent baby in its basket became the Royal Arches.

The story of El Capitan? *Tu-tok-a-nu'-la* rose when two bear cubs fell asleep on a sun-splashed rock after swimming in the Merced. The rock rose higher and higher, and the cubs were stranded on top. The "animal people" of *Ahwahnee*, from the mouse to the mountain lion, tried to jump up the sheer cliff to rescue them, but the only one to reach the summit was the measuring worm. The worm inched up over a long season, then brought the cubs down—in one version, safely, and in another, only their bones. The worm then climbed back up the monolith, stretched across the Valley to the south side, and then stretched back again. This weakened the walls so that portions crumbled, creating piles of talus on the Valley floor.

The name *Pohono* is preserved on the land, gracing the long trail that skims the southern rim of the Valley. *Po-ho-no* is the Ahwahneechee name for Bridalveil Fall. Now one of the premier destinations in the Valley, the waterfall was feared and avoided by the first people, who told of maidens that devoured those who came too close to the lake that was the source of the waterfall, and of a spirit with "the breath of a fatal wind" that haunted the fall itself.

In the Ahwahneechee tradition, the Lost Arrow, a spire located just east of Yosemite Falls that has been a siren for the park's big-wall climbers, was born of tragedy. The story can be told this way:

Kos-su-kah, a young chief of the Ahwahneechees, went into the mountains to hunt deer for his wedding feast. He was to marry Tee-hee-nay, fairest daughter of Ahwahnee. Kos-su-kah and his future bride agreed that once the hunt was complete, Kos-su-kah would climb to the great spire of rock that stands just east of Cho-lok (Yosemite Falls) at sunset, and launch an arrow to show the hunt had been successful. Tee-hee-nay would wait at the base of the cliff to mark the flight of the arrow, and carry news of the hunt's success back to the tribe.

After the hunt, Kos-su-kah stood at the great rock spire and readied the signal arrow, but he was so close to the cliff's edge that he tumbled off, plunging to his death. Tee-hee-nay waited in vain for sign of her lover's arrow, and when none came she followed the steep trail to the cliff top. There, with sobbing breath, she peered into the void and saw her lifeless lover's body on the rocks below. She built a signal fire to summon help from her tribe and, using ropes fashioned from tamarack and deerskin thongs, Kos-su-kah was lifted back to the rim.

Reunited, Tee-hee-nay embraced her fallen lover, and prayed for the Great Spirit to "take my breath so I may be with my husband-to-be." The Great Spirit, hearing her plea, did just that. The signal arrow Kos-su-kah fired in joyous celebration was never found. To honor the tragic lovers, the Ahwahneechee have since called the spire Hum-mo, "the Lost Arrow."

(Sources: Climber John Long, sacredtexts.com, interpretive ranger Phil Johnson, *Legends of the Yosemite Miwok*)

FROM AHWAHNEE TO YOSEMITE

The Ahwahneechee, like their brethren throughout California, would eventually be forced to cede control of their homeland to the white man. But not completely. The gold miners came and went, the Mariposa Battalion came and went, the US Cavalry came and went, the National Park Service came and stayed, and through that evolution, the Indians persevered. Although their villages were demolished or relocated, and they were no longer able to live a traditional lifestyle, they endured.

Having their *Ahwahnee* recognized as a national treasure—something to be conserved even as it was exploited—enabled the Indians to continue living in the Valley. They were confined to the park's designated Indian Village, their bark-and-brush homes replaced with more modern, if ramshackle, cabins, which was better than removal to reservation or rancheria, where many of California's surviving Indians ended up.

The men conformed to the new order by working for the park as laborers, guides, and ranch hands. One Yosemite man, Chris Brown, made a livelihood from his persona as Chief Lemee or Le-Me. Brown had learned the dances of his tribe as a boy, and for more than twenty years he would perform those dances (and, reportedly, some he just made up) for the entertainment of park visitors. He also demonstrated traditional hunting techniques, including flintknapping (the making of arrowheads from obsidian), and created recordings of traditional songs for the Yosemite Museum. He also built the sweathouse in the reconstructed Indian Village behind the museum.

Yosemite women proved adaptable as well. They found work in laundries, as housekeepers, and in child care, but they also developed a niche

Chris Brown, as Chief Lemee, dances in traditional Miwok ceremonial dress. PHOTO: R. A. ANDERSON, 1950. COURTESY OF THE YOSEMITE NATIONAL PARK ARCHIVES, MUSEUM, AND LIBRARY.

that would earn them some renown. No longer needed for utilitarian purposes, the baskets they wove were sold as souvenirs to the tourists who flocked to the park.

Among the basket weavers was Maggie Howard (*Ta-bu-ce*), who worked for many years at the park museum. Maggie also survived a harrowing accident in the high country, according to one historian. She and several family members were spending the night in a canyon above Yosemite Falls when a large tree fell onto their camp, killing her niece and badly injuring Maggie. She was left for dead under the fallen tree, and not rescued until the following day.

Lucy Telles also left a remarkable basket-weaving legacy, including the largest basket preserved in the Yosemite Museum. She passed her skills down: Her grandson, Ralph Parker, would marry Julia Domingues and bring her home to Yosemite. Here, grandmother Lucy would teach the young bride, now known as Julia Parker, how to weave. Julia would go on to become an Indian cultural demonstrator in the park like her grandmother-in-law, and, in turn, has taught her own daughter and granddaughter the traditions of basket-weaving. Julia's works—and through them, the legacy of Yosemite's Native peoples—are displayed in the Smithsonian Institution and have been presented to the Queen of England.

Through the middle of the twentieth century, the number of Indians calling Yosemite Valley home dwindled. The original Indian Village was replaced with a smaller village that included fifteen cabins with running water and bathroom facilities, and was occupied by about one hundred souls. But the cost of living in the park continued to take a toll. By 1969, so few Yosemite Indians remained that the newer village was dismantled. Today, no descendants of the Ahwahneechee call Yosemite home.

━━⌣━━

Julia Parker, sitting on the corner of the platform in the Yosemite Museum, has at her fingertips all the tools she needs to make a soaproot brush. Some are well worn, passed down from her teachers, and others are new, like the freshly harvested bulb. She peels a thicket of bristles from the root-ball; it looks like a brush from the outset. Fanning the fibrous mass across her thigh, she takes a bone awl and begins combing through it. The awl cleans the soil out of the fibers, she explains, adding that root hairs are dark because they've been stained by iron oxide in the soil. As she works, she tells the visitors who've gathered that the soap, from which the root takes its name, was used by the Ahwahneechee and other California Indians to clean things. And the juice of the root could "knock out" the fish swimming in a hole in the river, making them easy to catch.

The dogbane string she winds through the base of the brush has been cured for a year, like basket-making materials traditionally are. She stretches the string across her thigh, scrapes it lightly, then splits it with her teeth, bottom to top, "earth to sky."

Asked how long it would take her to make the brush, she comments, "We don't really think about the time." Asked by a young girl what the brush is for, she smiles, her eyes bird-bright. She picks up an older brush and runs it through her long, straight, gray-white hair.

"This is the way we comb our hair, comb our hair, comb our hair," she sings.

The Mariposa Battalion

THE MARIPOSA INDIAN WAR WAS, LIKE ALL AMERICAN INDIAN WARS, rooted in the desire to possess territory and power. But amazingly, given the value placed on the Yosemite Valley today, the land as a scenic wonder wasn't the primary motivation behind formation of the Mariposa Battalion. The miners and settlers who formed the battalion had no concept of *Ahwahnee*—of the bounty and beauty that the Valley's "first people" would eventually lose. The pioneers just wanted to make sure the Indians of the Sierra foothills and nearby flatlands were rounded up and locked away. If the Natives were confined to a reservation, they wouldn't be able to steal horses, rob stores, murder settlers, and inhibit access to mountain strongholds that might contain gold.

Manifest destiny, meet California.

THE WALKER EXPEDITION

While members of the Mariposa Battalion would be the first white men to enter the Yosemite Valley, it's generally agreed that fur trappers from an exploratory party led by American captain Joseph Walker were the first to see it.

It was 1833, and California was a Mexican frontier. Gold had yet to be discovered; at that time it was pelts—beaver pelts, in particular—that brought riches to the enterprising mountain man. If the abundance of game on America's Great Plains was any indication, the territories opening up to the west of the Rocky Mountains harbored great promise.

The Walker expedition hit the Sierra Nevada in October, just as winter descended. Hauling themselves and their pack animals across Sierran peaks and valleys was fraught; the men resorted to killing and eating a number of their travel-desiccated horses to survive, according to a narrative written by party member Zenas Leonard. Scouts were sent ahead to determine the safest, easiest passage across the range. Over the course of the crossing, these scouting parties brought back word of giant trees—the mighty sequoia—in what would become known as the Tuolumne Grove and the Merced Grove. At one point they would also encounter an Indian who, in shock, dropped his burden of acorns and fled; the trappers were delighted to consume the windfall.

Leonard also writes of encountering "deep chasms," where streams cut deeply into the granite before tumbling over precipices that "appeared to us to be more than a mile high." There was no safe way to drop into the chasms, which flowed westward toward the plain that Walker could see through his spyglass—the great Central Valley, full of forage for his animals and game for his hunters. So the Walker party skirted the voids—still no easy task, with Leonard recounting how the men had to "fasten ropes" around the horses to lower them safely down steep pitches on the descent.

When the party arrived in Monterey, capital of Alta California, the Mexican government—as it had done with another famous mountain man, Jedediah Smith—kicked Walker and his men out of its territory. And, like Smith, Walker took the long way around, so he could scout as much territory as possible for future expeditions. He headed south out of the San Joaquin Valley, following an Indian trail over the tail end of the Sierra Nevada into the Mojave Desert, near Death Valley. Walker Pass is named for the trapper; the route was used in subsequent years by settlers headed west into the Golden State, and is now a staging area for thru-hikers on the Pacific Crest Trail.

There's no written record, but the Indians living in the Yosemite Valley, thousands of feet below, knew of the Walker expedition's passage. If nothing else, the Native traveler who met Walker's scouts would have had something to say about how he lost his load of acorns on the trail. And Chief Tenaya of the Yosemite Indians would acknowledge, in the time of the Mariposa Indian War, that a party of white men had crossed the mountains north of the Valley before any set foot in the Valley proper.

There's some debate about whether Walker's expedition saw Yosemite Valley itself, or gazed down into the gorge of the Merced River near the

Yosemite Valley as seen from Union Point. PHOTO: CARLETON WATKINS. COURTESY OF THE YOSEMITE NATIONAL PARK ARCHIVES, MUSEUM, AND LIBRARY.

Cascades. There's also the record of a man named William Penn Abrams, who happened upon the Valley while tracking a grizzly bear. Abrams's description, from an October 1849 diary entry, is quoted by historian Hank Johnston: "Found our way to camp over an Indian trail that led past a valley enclosed by stupendous cliffs rising perhaps 3,000 feet from their base, and which gave us cause for wonder. Not far off a waterfall dropped from a cliff below three jagged peaks into the valley, which farther beyond, a rounded mountain stood, the valley side of which looked as though it had been sliced with a knife as one would slice a loaf of bread."

It's pretty clear Abrams was looking at the Cathedral Rocks, Bridalveil Fall, and Half Dome. But Abrams makes no mention of meeting the Yosemites, who resided, as yet unmolested, in the Valley at the time. And there's no record of Tenaya having seen Abrams and his companion.

But by that time the gold rush was well under way, and any crew traveling overland through the Sierra Nevada would have left a trace. It's fair to say the mountain Indians witnessed the passage of strangers in the high country long before the strangers came to stay.

THE BIGGER PICTURE

By the time of the Mariposa Indian War, nearly twenty years after Walker's expedition, the Sierra Miwok, including the residents of the Yosemite Valley, were well acquainted with the Americans settling the new state of California. The gold rush brought miners and their followers to the Sierra in a flood. The gold would eventually play out, but California's other attractions—its fertile soil, abundant lumber, amenable weather, spectacular scenery, and growing, self-propagating population of railroad barons, banking tycoons, mercantile moguls, water magnates, and captains of industry—would continue to fuel the influx.

Annexation of Alta California and other Mexican territories in the far West came fast on the heels of the discovery of gold in the Sierra foothills. Yosemite and everything surrounding it, from San Diego to the Oregon Territory, became part of the United States with the signing of the Treaty of Guadalupe Hidalgo in February 1848. Gold had been liberated from a millrace in Coloma in January of that year. Prior to the discovery, securing the Mexican territories had been mostly a strategic political move, with the expanding United States seeking to acquire, among other assets, coastal outposts established as part of the Spanish mission system, including ports in San Diego, Monterey, and San Francisco. The prospect of mineral riches only made the prize more desirable.

The tribes that had lived and camped in the Sierra for thousands of years had not consented to the Treaty of Guadalupe Hidalgo, had not participated in negotiations, and didn't value the gold that had been found in the foothills. Their ties to the land were practical and traditional. Starting with the arrival of the Spanish in the late eighteenth century, they had been forced to make quick and unimaginable transitions. Their numbers dwindled, the people dying of diseases they'd never been exposed to, starving as they were forced to relinquish hunting and gathering grounds, and dispersing into mission settlements where they served as neophytes. They had, throughout the colonial period, waged a number of violent rebellions, battling to hold on to their way of life.

Once word got out about California's gold, the changes became even more cataclysmic. Whatever the Spanish had failed to destroy, the new American onslaught would. Yes, they would ultimately lose the war, but California's tribal people weren't going down without a fight.

THE FORMATION OF THE MARIPOSA BATTALION

In the spirit of the times, James Savage was justified. Yosemite's Indians had attacked his property and committed murder. It was both his right and his duty to impose justice.

The Yosemites, like the other tribes of the southern Sierra and the San Joaquin Valley, were justified as well. Their homelands had been overrun in a few short years by prospectors who slaughtered game and cut down the oaks that provided acorns, the foundation of their diet. When the Yosemites took horses and provisions from the forty-niners, they were, as their chief Tenaya would explain, simply attempting to replace what had been taken from them.

Conflicts on the Mariposa frontier, known as the "Southern Mines," dated back to the beginning of the gold rush, and involved more than just the mountain tribe. But the tipping point for the Mariposa Indian War would be a raid by the Yosemites on Savage's trading post on the Fresno River in December 1850.

Savage was a central player in the Mariposa region. His arrival pre-dated the gold rush; having lost his wife and child on the overland journey to California in 1846, he would spend several years as a soldier of fortune before, like so many others, catching gold fever. According to Carl Parcher Russell, author of *One Hundred Years in Yosemite*, Savage demonstrated an "aptitude" for languages, which enabled him to communicate with the local Indians and establish trade with them. He would come to employ Indians to bring placer gold collected in foothills streams to his trading posts, where it was exchanged for food and other goods. In Russell's narrative Savage is described as a respected "white chief" among Indians of the foothills and neighboring flatlands. He would also, by all accounts, make a fortune off his traffic with Indians, as well as with the miners who traded gold for Savage's goods.

But not all the mountain Indians were compliant and respectful, and Savage was not universally generous in his dealings with those Indians.

Russell describes an 1850 raid on Savage's first trading post, located at the mouth of the South Fork of the Merced River. In the aftermath, Savage vowed to "get into the den of the thieving murderers. If I ever have a chance I will smoke out [the Yosemites] from their holes, where they are thought to be so secure."

Savage established two new trading posts, one on Mariposa Creek and one on the Fresno River. But tensions between tribes seeking to retain their territorial claims and white settlers seeking to usurp those claims escalated over the ensuing year. It wasn't just the Yosemites who proved difficult; the Chowchillas also were suspicious and rebellious, as were the Chukchansi, the Kaweahs, and others.

When the Yosemites raided Savage's new trading post on Fresno River, the sole survivor reported that the store was destroyed and three men killed. With that, in Russell's words, "The Mariposa Indian War was on."

Savage and Mariposa sheriff James Burney moved quickly to muster men to bring the culprits to justice. Their efforts were backed by the state of California, with Governor John McDougal authorizing the formation of a 204-man force to defend the Southern Mines. The federal government also got involved, sending commissioners to Mariposa to establish treaties with the tribes and move them onto a reservation on the Fresno River near the foothills. When some of the tribes, including the Yosemites, refused to treat with the federal commission, the battalion was authorized to bring them in.

The Mariposa Battalion was composed of three companies, which followed different rivers into the high Sierra to subdue and "escort" the mountain Indians to the reservation on the Fresno. The company detached to head up the Merced into the stronghold of the Yosemite included Dr. Lafayette H. Bunnell, whose *The Discovery of the Yosemite* is acknowledged as a definitive account of the exploits of the Mariposa Battalion in the spring of 1851.

THE FIRST FORAY

It was late March 1851 when Savage's company set out for the Valley. They encountered rain and then snow as they ascended, which would play into how negotiations proceeded when they encountered the Yosemite Indians in the high country.

The campaign started with a success for Savage's company, as it captured an Indian village near Wawona. From there, runners were dispatched to the villages of the Yosemite. The message: The Yosemites were to abandon their mountain abode and consent to treating with the federal commissioners and living on the reservation. They were told that they "would there be furnished with food and clothing, and receive protection," Bunnell wrote, "but if they did not come in, he [Savage] should make war upon them until he destroyed them all."

The next day, Tenaya (spelled *Ten-ie-ya* by Bunnell), the "old chief of the Yosemites," appeared in the company camp. Tenaya told Savage that the Yosemites did not want anything that the white men offered; that in their valley, they had all they needed. "Go, then," the chief told the major. "Let us remain in the mountains where we were born; where the ashes of our fathers have been given to the winds."

But Savage had a retort. "If you and your people have all you desire," he asked Tenaya, "why do you steal our horses and mules? Why do you rob the miners' camps? Why do you murder the white men, and plunder and burn their houses?"

The old chief considered Savage's complaint, then explained that his men thought of the prospectors as enemies, and, in the Yosemite tradition, it was not wrong to take the property of enemies. This would stop now that they knew better. But, he continued, the Yosemites would not agree to leave their valley. Only in the Valley, he said, would they be able to defend themselves.

Savage stood firm. Bunnell describes more debate, but in the end Tenaya agreed to return to his people and advise them to head down the mountain with the white men.

Tenaya did not deliver as expected. Several days passed, and the Yosemites did not appear. Eventually the old chief returned, and explained that the snows were too deep for his people to come down. Savage and the company captains, however, were skeptical and tired of waiting, so they headed up to the Valley to forcibly bring the Yosemites out.

On the way, while "wallowing" in snowpack five feet deep, the company met a band of Yosemites, seventy-two in all, who intended to comply with American orders.

Yosemite Falls. COURTESY OF THE YOSEMITE NATIONAL PARK ARCHIVES, MUSEUM, AND LIBRARY

Tenaya agreed to accompany this group of seventy-two down to the reservation. But Savage, not believing that all the Yosemites had left the Valley, pressed onward and upward with a smaller contingent of men. "They *will* come with me if I find them," he told the chief. Tenaya replied that his tribe was not as numerous as Savage believed, and that the younger members had crossed the mountains to join the Mono Paiutes on the east side of the Sierra. Why would the young men of his tribe, he asked the major, consent "to be yarded like horses and cattle" on a reservation when the mountains gave them everything they needed?

YOSEMITE FOR THE FIRST TIME

"None but those who have visited this most wonderful valley, can even imagine the feelings with which I looked upon the view that was there presented. The grandeur of the scene was but softened by the haze that hung over the valley,—light as gossamer—and by the clouds which partially dimmed the higher cliffs and mountains. This obscurity of vision but increased the awe with which I beheld it, and as I looked, a peculiar exalted sensation seemed to fill my whole being, and I found my eyes in tears with emotion."

This is how Dr. Bunnell described what he and his companions saw when they entered the Yosemite Valley in the late afternoon of March 21, 1851. They'd reached Inspiration Point, and before them El Capitan caught the sun, and Bridalveil Fall caught the wind. It was—and is—a stunning sight, one that never fails to inspire.

In camp that night, Bunnell would propose the name "Yo-sem-it-y" for the Valley, arguing that the tribal name, which translated to "grizzly bear," couldn't be more American, and "that by so doing, the name of the tribe of Indians which we met leaving their homes in this valley, perhaps never to return, would be perpetuated." This suggestion met some resistance, with one man declaring "Devil take the Indians and their names!" But a vote was taken, and Yo-sem-it-y won.

Ahwahnee, however, was lost. Bunnell recounts Chief Tenaya's "prophecy": The old chief, when young, had been told by an Ahwahneechee elder that, so long as the entrance to the Valley was hidden and defended—so long as the "horsemen of the lowlands" did not enter—the people of the

Valley would be safe. Should the gateway be breeched, "his tribe would soon be scattered and destroyed, or his people be taken captive, and he himself be the last chief in *Ah-wah-ne*."

This, Tenaya explained, was why the Yosemites had a reputation for fierceness: They had to be ferocious in defense of their "deep grassy valley." The prophecy also goes a long way toward explaining why Tenaya postponed and diverted the militia, telling the major one thing and doing another, in a way the white men deemed "cunning." Because he was an old man, Bunnell writes, Tenaya's passion for war had faded. But he could still protect *Ahwahnee* by agreeing to a treaty with the Americans, and hopefully keeping the stronghold in the possession of his people.

The Valley, however, had finally, formally, been penetrated. The Yosemites scattered through the talus and climbed into the wilderness, abandoning their villages, their caches of acorns, their basketware, their huts and roundhouses and sweat lodges, to avoid capture by Savage and his men. Scouts sent deeper into the canyons returned empty-handed and downcast—in spite of having hiked alongside Vernal and Nevada Falls, and up into Little Yosemite—for they were unable to locate the rest of the tribe.

Among those who fled the Valley, estimated to number two hundred, was *To-tu-ya* (Foaming Waters), granddaughter of Chief Tenaya. Many years later, when she was called Maria Lebrado, the granddaughter would return to the Valley to see again what she'd been forced to leave when she was a girl. Russell, who interviewed Lebrado in 1929, would remark that she "recalled [Major Savage] as something [of] a thorn in her flesh." The party did succeed in finding one refugee, according to Bunnell: an ancient woman hiding in a cave who was too old to climb the rocks to escape.

Major Savage decided to abandon the Valley—for a while, at least. Hoping to flush the remaining Yosemites out by starving them, he ordered the villages and food caches destroyed. His foray wasn't a complete loss; he still had a contingent of Yosemites, as well as captives from other tribes, to deliver to the reservation. He left these Indians under the supervision of one of his subordinates, Captain Boling, and returned to the battalion's headquarters ahead of the main party. Captain Boling, unfortunately for the major, would later arrive at headquarters with a single Indian. He confessed to having fallen asleep while on guard and, while unobserved, the captives had slipped away, fleeing back into the mountains, back to the Yosemite.

The Second Foray

The second advance into the Yosemite Valley was led by the same Captain Boling who had fallen asleep on the job in March. Major Savage, Bunnell wrote, had all confidence that such an oversight would not be repeated.

Upon reaching the Valley, the company found the first few huts they encountered abandoned. But then a group of five Indians was spotted across the river near El Capitan. The Merced was high, so it took a while for the militia to find a reasonable ford, but once they did, they set out in pursuit of the five Yosemites.

The Indians were overtaken near what is now called the Three Brothers, so named, according to Bunnell, because three of the captured Yosemite scouts were sons of Chief Tenaya's. The old chief and the remaining Yosemites had fled hurriedly upon the militia's approach, and the five had remained to track the advance. The young men told their captors that Tenaya would come down to make peace if his safety was secured, and indicated that the Yosemites had taken refuge in what would become known as Tenaya Canyon. Bunnell was a member of the battalion scouting party, which included two of the captured Yosemites, that headed up into the canyon to retrieve the chief and his tribe. But the party was forced to retreat when the Yosemites began rolling stones down upon them, badly injuring one militiaman. Recognizing the danger, Captain Boling decided to wait on Tenaya, hoping the chief would keep his promise to surrender.

Tenaya did come down, but only to tragedy and despair. The following day, while another party went up into the canyon to parley with Tenaya, some of the militiamen convinced one of the captives to demonstrate his skill with bow and arrow. The target was placed farther and farther away, and as the arrows had to be retrieved for subsequent shots, the Yosemite bowman was employed in looking for them. He broke away, escaping up into what would become known as Indian Canyon.

Captain Boling, "who was peculiarly sensitive on the subject of escaped prisoners," was "greatly annoyed" by this development, according to Bunnell. To prevent their escape, the two remaining Indians, including Tenaya's youngest son, were tied up back to back and lashed to a tree. But the two were able to free themselves, and as they fled, Tenaya's son was shot down. The other was able to escape. Bunnell and his captain determined this to be, essentially, a murder: "The Indians had been permitted to untie themselves, and an opportunity had been given them to attempt to escape in order to fire upon them, expecting to kill them both."

When the scouting party returned, having captured Tenaya, he was confronted with the body of his beloved son. His grief was profound. Bunnell reports that the father was held captive while the search for the rest of the band continued, without success. But when the chance arose, the old chief attempted escape, fleeing to the Merced. Upon recapture, as recorded by Bunnell, Tenaya unleashed his wrath upon Boling:

> *"Kill me, sir Captain! Yes, kill me, as you killed my son; as you would kill my people if they were to come to you! You would kill all my race if you had the power. Yes, sir, American, you can now tell your warriors to kill the old chief; you have made me sorrowful, my life dark; you killed the child of my heart, why not kill the father? But wait a little; when I am dead I will call to my people to come to you, I will call louder than you have had me call; that they shall hear me in their sleep, and come to avenge the death of their chief and his son. Yes, sir, American, my spirit will make trouble for you and your people, as you have caused trouble to me and my people. With the wizards, I will follow the white men and make them fear me. You may kill me, sir, Captain, but you shall not live in peace. I will follow in your foot-steps, I will not leave my home, but be with the spirits among the rocks, the waterfalls, in the rivers and in the winds; wheresoever you go I will be with you. You will not see me, but you will fear the spirit of the old chief, and grow cold. The great spirits have spoken! I am done."*

In the days that followed, Captain Boling led a contingent into the high country and captured a small band of Yosemites near a lovely lake

Tuolumne Meadows. COURTESY OF THE YOSEMITE NATIONAL PARK ARCHIVES, MUSEUM, AND LIBRARY.

surrounded by snowbound peaks. Bunnell would call the lake "Tenaya," and this would stick. But the old chief, who had accompanied the militiamen into the high park, told him, "It already has a name; we call it *Py-we-ack*," which has been translated, perhaps erroneously, as "lake of the shining rocks."

The young chief of the starving band, which included four of Tenaya's wives, was willing to submit to Captain Boling's demands and descend to the reservation. "Where can we now go that the Americans will not follow us?" he said. "Where can we make our homes, that you will not find us?"

Captain Boling led the Yosemites down out of the mountains and onto the reservation. "We reached the Fresno without the loss of a captive," Bunnell wrote. "And as we turned them over to the agent, we were formally commended for the success of the expedition."

Disbanded

In July 1851, having accomplished its mission, the Mariposa Battalion was disbanded. The combative Indians of the foothills and the San Joaquin River valley had been subdued and removed to the Fresno reservation. The Southern Mines were now free to be exploited without threat of conflict.

The Yosemites were also disbanded, scattered between the Fresno reservation and the camps of neighboring tribes, including the Mono Paiutes and the Sierra Miwoks of the Tuolumne. The breach of *Ahwahnee* was complete, prospectors and the curious descending on the Valley in ever-greater numbers.

Chief Tenaya and his family were permitted to return to Yosemite just months after they were brought to the reservation, having made promises not to cause any trouble.

But there would be further conflict. Two miners would be killed by Yosemites in 1852; in their defense, the Indians would claim the land was still theirs, and that they had the right to defend it. Those Indians would be executed for their crimes. In the wake of the killings, Tenaya and his people fled over the mountains and found sanctuary with the Mono on the east side of the Sierra.

But the Valley called the chief and his remaining people home one last time. They ventured back into *Ahwahnee* in 1853 and established a small village among the rock spires and cathedrals. They wouldn't be there long. The story goes that a small party of young men headed back down to the Mono camp and stole horses, which they led back to the Yosemite village. There, the Yosemites feasted on horseflesh. The Mono retaliated by attacking the Yosemite camp, and in the skirmish Tenaya was stoned to death. Others in the small band were also killed, and the rest fled.

As for Major Savage, he would be killed a year after the Mariposa Battalion was disbanded, shot down by Walter Harvey, whom he accused of massacring Indians on the recently established reservation. His death, according to Russell, would incite "great" grief among the reservation's Natives.

By 1855, the few Indians that remained on the Fresno reservation were allowed to leave. This included a small number of Yosemites, who climbed back into the Yosemite Valley. They found it changed, and their existence there was hardscrabble. Yosemite's future guardian, Galen Clark, describes a "precarious and transitory" people. Livestock fed on the acorns that had once been their staple food, so they suffered from starvation; some of the women became "commercial property"; and they acquired the "vices" of the settlers while on the reservation, including gambling and liquor. By the turn of the twentieth century, according to Clark, only a handful of Yosemites who could remember the Valley before its "discovery" remained. The last would be Chief Tenaya's granddaughter, Maria Lebrado. When she died in 1931, she took with her the last memories of *Ahwahnee* before the Mariposa Battalion.

The Cutting Edge:
The Creation and Evolution of
Yosemite National Park

In a country as vast and new as the United States in the mid-1800s, the idea that landscapes might need preservation was absurd. Wilderness was limitless, needed to be tamed, and was full of resources to exploit.

And then came Yosemite.

People looked on the Yosemite Valley and the Mariposa Grove of Big Trees with a possessive eye. But they didn't only want to own; they wanted to share. California was a newborn state full of fortune-seekers, adventurers, and freethinkers, and Yosemite inspired in them a cutting-edge and farsighted vision for a newfound national wonder.

The idea was to set aside these remarkable landscapes, undisturbed and unexploited, as a public park. The traditional commercial interests that fueled Manifest Destiny were trumped. There might be gold; there was certainly timber; the meadows could be grazed; the critters could be hunted. But more than that, there was beauty. There were waterfalls and cliffs and trees so huge and old they defied imagination. Intangibles, almost miraculously, became more valuable than hard rock and lumber.

The nation created something entirely new to protect Yosemite: a national park system. And while Yellowstone would become America's first official national park, it was only by virtue of a technicality. Yosemite got the nod years earlier. And Yosemite would continue to be the crucible of the national park idea, for better or for worse, into modern times.

THE YOSEMITE GRANT ACT

Be it enacted by the Senate and House of Representatives of the United States of America in Congress assembled, [t]hat there shall be, and is hereby, granted to the State of California the "cleft" or "gorge" in the granite peak of the Sierra Nevada Mountains, situated in the county of Mariposa, in the State aforesaid, and the headwaters of the Merced River, and known as the Yo-Semite Valley with the stipulation, nevertheless, that the said State shall accept this grant upon the express conditions that the premises shall be held for public use, resort, and recreation; shall be inalienable for all time.

—FROM THE YOSEMITE GRANT ACT, SIGNED INTO LAW BY
PRESIDENT ABRAHAM LINCOLN ON JUNE 30, 1864

After the surveys were said and done, the Yosemite Grant included about 36,000 acres, measuring about fifteen miles along the length of the Yosemite Valley, and reaching a mile back on either side from the "edge of the precipice." The Mariposa Grove grant encompassed four sections, or about 2,600 acres. All this in the gold-rich Sierra Nevada, just thirteen years after the Mariposa Battalion "discovered" the Valley.

The Yosemite act, granting the Valley and grove to California for protection as parkland, was inspired by threats that materialized almost immediately upon the arrival of Americans in the region. In addition to the unprecedented natural beauty, which could be leveraged in tourist trade, Yosemite also possessed mineral wealth and timber. Californians who wanted to preserve the Valley would have to act quickly to protect it from Californians who wanted to exploit it.

James Hutchings, a gold miner turned publisher, gets much credit for bringing the natural values of Yosemite to the attention of the nation. His motives were not altruistic: He laid claim to a plot of land within the Valley and established a business there, then fought hard to hang on to that land once the Valley was set aside as a park.

Yosemite as park had other champions as well, among them Horace Greeley, publisher of the *New York Tribune*; Reverend Thomas Starr King, who vacationed in Yosemite in 1860, and wrote about the Valley for the

El Capitan. PHOTO: R. H. ANDERSON, 1934. COURTESY OF THE YOSEMITE NATIONAL PARK ARCHIVES, MUSEUM, AND LIBRARY.

Boston Evening Transcript; and Frederick Law Olmsted, who had already distinguished himself as the designer of New York's Central Park. Images of Yosemite created by artists like Thomas Ayres and Albert Bierstadt, and photographers like Carleton Watkins and Charles L. Weed, helped people far distant visualize the waterfalls and monoliths. Americans quickly became enamored of a place most of them would never see. They were also inspired to protect it from the ravages that natural wonders in their own backyards, like Niagara Falls, had endured, having fallen into private hands and been pieced out and monetized, with degradation of their intrinsic beauty one of the sad results.

Luckily, the most obvious resources that Yosemite and the Mariposa Grove might offer enterprising Californians happened not to materialize. Later in the nineteenth century a vein of silver ore would be mined in the high country—land not included in the Yosemite Grant, but later incorporated into Yosemite National Park. But at the time the Yosemite Grant Act was proposed, no one had unearthed enough precious metal within the Valley to bring on a rush. And the sequoia, as a timber product, would prove itself prone to splintering and shattering upon being downed or milled, although men would still decimate groves in an effort to make it work.

Histories point to a letter from Israel Ward Raymond, a steamship captain who visited the Valley in the early 1860s, to John Conness, a onetime forty-niner turned California state legislator turned US senator, as the impetus for the bill that would protect both the Yosemite Valley and the Mariposa Grove. Conness would argue that both valley and grove were, "for all public purposes worthless, but constitute, perhaps, some of the greatest wonders of the world. The object and purpose is to make a grant to the State, on the stipulation contained in the bill that the property shall be inalienable forever, and preserved and improved as a place of public resort."

Congress and President Lincoln would agree. Yosemite and the Mariposa Grove of Big Trees had made history as the first "national" park.

California in Charge

There were good reasons to let California take charge of Yosemite and the Mariposa Grove in those years, as opposed to having them fall under national oversight. First, the country was still embroiled in the Civil War. That Congress and the president took the time to consider and sign off on the Yosemite Grant Act in 1864 was remarkable given the huge losses and profound issues being grappled with at the time.

In addition, nothing like a national park had been seen before. There were no mechanisms in place to manage such a beast. Yosemite would become, in many instances and on many levels, a testing ground for concepts of preservation and conservation that had never before been put into practice. Having the state take those challenges on, in that time, was the easy answer.

Preservation and *conservation.* The words are often used interchangeably, but they connote significantly different actions. Simply put, as defined by the National Park Service, conservation seeks the *proper use of nature*, while preservation seeks *protection of nature from use.* Neither idea is better than the other, but the two present a push-me pull-you: How do you preserve nature without conservation, and how do you conserve nature without preservation? It's a balancing act, and in Yosemite the balance has swung back and forth since the park's inception—and continues to swing. In the administration of the Yosemite Grant Act, conflicts between proponents of preservation and proponents of conservation were given a political forum.

Considering how ponderous most legislation that moves through Congress is in modern times, the Yosemite Grant Act is simple. No pork attached: The act deals only with establishing the Yosemite and Mariposa reserves. It also established a board of commissioners, overseen by the state governor, to administer the grant. The first board included some of the biggest boosters of Yosemite's natural values: Olmsted; Josiah Whitney, California's state geologist (and other members of the parties that first surveyed Yosemite and the high Sierra); Raymond, who wrote the letter that spurred the congressional act; and Galen Clark, who lived and breathed Yosemite. The guardian was the commission's man on the ground, the enforcer overseeing the execution of commission orders. Clark was Yosemite's first and best guardian, holding the post for the first fourteen years of the grant, and then for a second term after a turbulent hiatus.

In addition to setting the Valley and grove aside for public use and recreation, the Yosemite Grant Act also allowed for ten-year leases on property within the park, with revenues from said leases "to be expended in the preservation and improvement" of the reserve. But the act does not specify what those uses could be; that would be determined by the board of commissioners. Issues of preservation versus conservation were not addressed at the federal level. Instead, in those first years, just how Yosemite would be curated was left up to California.

The frontier state, just more than a decade old, was ill prepared to protect the Yosemite Valley and Mariposa Grove from the depredations of uses already established within the grant: homesteading, sheepherding, mining, timber cutting, and the tourist trade. The biggest issues then, as now, were people and money. How many people could the grant accommodate before its natural values began to degrade? What was the best way to get those people into and out of the Valley and the grove? What were people going to be permitted to do, and not do, within the grant? How was the state going to pay for any improvements needed? The only way to find out was to carry on.

The ten-year leases ensured income to support improvements, though that income would prove inadquate as increased use necessitated more expensive infrastructure. The leases also meant turnover among the purveyors of services to tourists. Hoteliers and the builders of toll roads were most impacted by the policy. Applications to operate an inn or run a road in the Yosemite Grant had to be made to the board of commissioners, and were subject to approval by the state legislature. And the commission's view of what was good for the Valley didn't always jibe with the views of its residents.

Subject to this system, one of the Yosemite Valley's biggest promoters would become one of its biggest and sorest losers. Within ten years of the signing of the act, the government began reclaiming private inholdings within the Valley. James Hutchings operated his hotel on a parcel that had been used for that purpose before the grant was established (though his personal claim on the land essentially coincided with passage of the act). He intended to keep operating without conforming to the leasing rules imposed by the act, and enlisted another pre-grant Valley resident,

James Lamon, to join him in his administrative and legal protests. When Hutchings and the commissioners couldn't come to terms, the commission leased Hutchings's hotel to another party.

Hutchings refused to submit. A bitter, years-long battle moved through the state legislature and into the courts. Hutchings won the argument in the legislature, which was sympathetic to his claims given his enthusiastic promotion of the Valley, but the idea that private property could be held within a state (or national) park ran contrary to the idea of such a park being preserved for all people. Fencing, for example, was cited as one way the public could be excluded from its inalienable right to enjoy the Valley. Given the terms of the grant, Hutchings and Lamon had no legal standing. Still, Hutchings took the case all the way to the Supreme Court, where he finally lost. He eventually left the Valley to pursue business interests elsewhere. But he'd be back, to serve as Yosemite's guardian in one instance, and finally, to die and be buried there.

As the Hutchings case demonstrates, the Yosemite Grant was not immune to the vagaries of politics, business, and finance. For example, competing demands for usage and rights led to conflict on wagon-road access to the Valley. The Coulterville Road and the Big Oak Flat Road would touch down on the Yosemite Valley floor within a month of each other, but only the company that had built the Coulterville Road had gone through the Yosemite commission for permission. The Big Oak Flat company, eager to cash in on tourists headed to the Valley floor more quickly, instead solicited and won approval for its road through the state legislature. Eventually the Big Oak Flat Road would outcompete the Coulterville Road, and the builders of the Coulterville route would sue. In the end all toll roads and trails would be acquired by the grant, allowing free passage into the reserve.

In 1880, in the aftermath of a state election and political restructuring, the original members of the Yosemite Commission were ousted and replaced with a new slate. The changes, according to historian Hank Johnston, proved controversial. The new commissioners got along better with members of California's legislature, which was "dominated by men favorable to the Southern Pacific Railroad," and thus were able to secure additional funding for improvements of roads and trails within the grant. Meanwhile, the former commissioners refused to acknowledge their removal. That disagreement, too, wound through the courts.

The reserve got new guardians in those years as well, among them James Hutchings. Despite his intimate knowledge of, and history in, the Yosemite Valley, his tenure lasted only four years. His removal was due, in part, to what Johnston calls his "tactless, imperious attitude, which irritated residents and commissioners alike." The next two guardians also held office for only a short time, earning the enmity of residents and commissioners for their poor stewardship. In 1889, just before the trajectory of Yosemite's development was altered yet again, the Yosemite Commission turned back to the dedicated and inspirational Galen Clark, reinstating him as guardian with the justifiable expectation that he, given his long history in the park, would instill some semblance of peace.

YOSEMITE NATIONAL PARK

The Yosemite Grant Act was a one-and-only piece of legislation. Congress had to come to grips with the idea that there were other landscapes on the American continent worthy of Yosemite-style preservation within years of passing the act. The bounty of Yellowstone, and the threats it faced, forced the nation's hand. But there was a wrinkle: Wyoming was still a territory; there was no state to oversee the reserve. De facto, Yellowstone became the first national park in 1872.

And then the lobbying for additional parks began. Its roots were in the American West, but the national parks movement would gain momentum on many fronts over the years, from Acadia to Mount Rainier; from the Everglades to the Grand Canyon; from the mountains of northern Montana to the ruins of Mesa Verde in the desert Southwest.

The nascent Yosemite National Park had a lobby as well. Preservation of the Valley and the Mariposa Grove was all well and good, but it was clear to anyone who understood the broader landscape that the watershed of the Merced, with its "fountains" on the crest of the Sierra Nevada, as well as the stunning landscapes of Tuolumne Meadows, the Tuolumne River, and the Hetch Hetchy Valley, should also be preserved. A chorus for a bigger, all-encompassing Yosemite National Park rang out, with the powerful voice of John Muir at the fore, Robert Underwood Johnson, publisher of *Century* magazine, providing a stage for the campaign, and the backbeat of the Yosemite commission, which had advocated for an expansion of the park for years.

President Benjamin Harrison signed the legislation authorizing the "Yosemite forest reserve," later to be called Yosemite National Park, on October 1, 1890. Legislation protecting the General Grant forest reserve, in what would become Sequoia & Kings Canyon National Park, was signed that same day. The new Yosemite reserve included more than 1,500 square miles surrounding the Valley, though the Mariposa Grove of Big Trees lay outside the boundary.

Seventeen years would pass before the Yosemite Grant would be folded into Yosemite National Park. John Muir and the Sierra Club spearheaded the movement advocating recession of the grant from state to federal control. Muir presented the case to President Theodore

John Muir and President Theodore Roosevelt ride through the Yosemite Valley.
A SOUTHERN PACIFIC RAILROAD PHOTOGRAPH, 1903. COURTESY OF THE YOSEMITE NATIONAL PARK ARCHIVES, MUSEUM, AND LIBRARY

Roosevelt over the course of a much-celebrated three-day camping junket in the Yosemite Valley and surrounding parklands. Advocacy for the recession was bolstered by continuing controversies surrounding California's administration of the Yosemite Grant. Securing funds for necessary infrastructure—maintenance of roads, trails, bridges, and buildings—was difficult to squeeze from the state legislature. Federal oversight of the grant—which had been, after all, established at that level—seemed a logical way to curb the plague of ongoing lawsuits and allegations of mismanagement, neglect, and favoritism in the "state" park. President Roosevelt signed the act unifying the Yosemite Grant and the surrounding national forest reserve in June 1906.

With the establishment of the national park and the incorporation of Yosemite Valley and the Mariposa Grove within its boundaries, preservation and conservation of Yosemite's resources were transformed. The state ceded oversight to the nation, which stepped forward with a unique management solution. The vehicle seems unlikely in a modern context, but at the time, it was clearly the best choice. The US Army was in charge.

THE ERA OF THE CAVALRY

Cavalry units of the US Army patrolled Yosemite National Park from 1891 to 1916, when the National Park Service was established. Their presence predated recession, but military oversight influenced preservation and conservation within the Yosemite Grant even as it focused on the surrounding parklands.

The soldiers dispatched from the Presidio of San Francisco for summer duty in the new parks of the Sierra Nevada—Yosemite and Sequoia—were well prepared to take on the challenges of a wilderness assignment, according to Yosemite interpretive ranger Shelton Johnson. Yes, they were trained warriors, but in the tradition of the times, officers who attended West Point studied botany, biology, and geology, which enabled them to better navigate the social and physical challenges posed by new environments, and to catalog the resources they encountered there.

Patrolling the new national parks, was, clearly, a peacetime occupation, but not without its challenges. The units assigned to Yosemite over the years found themselves dealing with a confounding variety of

Troops from the Sixth Cavalry pose on and around the Fallen Monarch in the Mariposa Grove of Big Trees. PHOTO: M. DIXON, 1899. COURTESY OF THE YOSEMITE NATIONAL PARK ARCHIVES, MUSEUM, AND LIBRARY.

assignments: finding lost hikers, road and trail construction and repair, firefighting, planting fish, catching poachers, monitoring grazing, and coping with the arrival of automobiles. The observation of one soldier on the difficulty of enforcing park rules, in this case with regard to poaching, encapsulates the most difficult aspect of the mission: its size. The soldier would note that "the difficulty of catching persons having and using firearms is great, owing to the fact that there are so many ways of entering and leaving the park."

Despite the challenges, one member of a company attached to the Fourth US Cavalry, which patrolled the high country beyond the Valley rim, described the work in a letter to park superintendent C. G. Thomson in 1932 as "a very pleasant assignment."

Frank Harkness was a member of the Utah Volunteer Cavalry, which took over the patrol after the Fourth Cavalry was sent to the Philippines in 1898. Dispatched into the high country to protect the mountain meadows from encroaching sheepherders, Harkness described the army's tactics: "Sometimes the herder was arrested, the bells removed from the sheep, the bands scattered, and a long trek made into headquarters and Wawona. By the time the trial was over, the sheep were so scattered that it was often impossible to save any number of them. At other times the sheep and herder were driven across to the opposite boundary in a fatiguing march which resulted in great loss and inconvenience to the herder."

His Yosemite assignment apparently agreed with Harkness as well; he noted that he received a letter from a female admirer who wrote: "[Y]ou did look like a sack of flour on your horse the day you left Salt Lake. Now I must say you came back riding like a Major-general."

An article published in the *Overland Monthly* in 1899, titled "Uncle Sam's Troopers in the National Parks of California," also captures the diversity of issues soldiers dealt with in those years. "In the Yosemite, some of the troopers are constantly kept busy in removing the marks of the tourist and the advertiser. All appeals to public favor which can be made on bits of wood and tin and muslin are destroyed almost as soon as created," the author writes. In another instance, soldiers encountered a "well-known society man of San Francisco, in search of novel sensations," who was so annoyed by people asking him questions about his solo Yosemite explorations that he pretended to be deaf and mute, responding "by using the deaf and dumb alphabet as he strode along. A well-meaning trooper endeavored to arrest him as a lunatic at large, when the member of the four hundred suddenly found his voice."

Among the troops assigned to patrol the new national parks were the Buffalo Soldiers, African-American companies with their origins dating back to the Civil War. These companies were deployed westward to fight in the Indian Wars; according to the park service they were "given the name Buffalo Soldiers by the Cheyenne and other Plains Indians who saw a resemblance between their dark, curly hair and the matted cushion between the horns of the buffalo." They also fought in the Philippines during the Spanish-American War. Stationed at the Presidio, the Ninth Cavalry and the Twenty-Fourth Mounted Infantry were dispatched to both the Yosemite and Sequoia reserves. Though racism made their position of authority tenuous at best, despite their military authority and the

The Twenty-Fourth Mounted Infantry on patrol in Yosemite's backcountry.
PHOTO: CELIA CROCKER THOMPSON, 1899. COURTESY OF THE YOSEMITE NATIONAL PARK
ARCHIVES, MUSEUM, AND LIBRARY.

honor of their service, the Buffalo Soldiers proved themselves "simultaneously strong *and* diplomatic to fulfill the duties of their job but to avoid giving offense." They had to give orders to people who were not accustomed to taking orders from African Americans, notes Ranger Johnson. "It's pretty amazing that they were doing what they were doing."

Soldiers patrolled the high country in the high season, from April through October, then retreated to the Presidio for the winter, with two "forest rangers" stationed in the park in the slower months. In the early years, under the command of Captain A. E. Wood, the cavalry was headquartered near Wawona, outside the Yosemite Grant. California was still in charge of the Valley at that time, and the army had little say in activities there. But the commanders—many captains, majors, and lieutenant colonels would hold the post over the years—were acting park superintendents, and once the Yosemite Grant was re-ceded from the state, they oversaw administration of the entire park. The issues they dealt with were cataloged in annual Superintendent's Reports. The report from 1912 offers a snapshot of what was tackled in that era, covering grazing, fires, game, fish, fences, patented lands, telephone service, roads, trails, bridges, concessions, hotels and camps, San Francisco's water supply (building a dam in the Hetch Hetchy Valley was in the works at the time), buildings, power plants, water supply, sanitation, deaths, Camp Yosemite, visitors, cost estimates, and recommendations. Camp Yosemite, on the Valley floor, had become US Army headquarters in May 1907; also known as "Fort Yosemite," the troops and officers were housed in tents, and the enclave was outfitted with all the necessities, including a blacksmith, stables, and a mess hall. It would be abandoned in 1913, as the army relinquished Yosemite to the National Park Service, which was beginning to take form.

DRAWING THE LINES

As part of the act of recession, Yosemite National Park's boundaries were redrawn. According to environmental historian Alfred Runte, Major Hiram Chittenden of the US Army Corps of Engineers, Frank Bond of the US General Land Office, and Robert Marshall of the US Geological Survey were among those who took on the monumental task of sussing out what was public land and what was private within the boundaries of the new park, including defining inholdings. The balancing act would result in the loss of more than five hundred square miles of the 1890 reserve.

Yosemite Valley and the Mariposa Grove of Big Trees were the prize on the public side; tracts of land opened to logging, mining, and tourism were the prize for private companies. The impacts on the ecosystem were profound, as the interests of the "private domain" imprinted the wilderness just outside the park's boundaries with clear-cuts, rail lines, mine tailings, and roadways. Among the biggest beneficiaries of the recession was the timber industry. The Yosemite Lumber Company, incorporated in 1910, established lumber camps throughout the greater Yosemite region—including one near the Merced Grove, and another at Crane Flat—and opened up tracts south and east of El Portal.

This wouldn't be the first time the park gained or lost ground. Wawona was incorporated into Yosemite in 1932, with the exception of private inholdings, and Foresta, a township platted in the 1920s, was also brought under the park's purview, but again, some of its cottages remained private property. Trades and purchases would also bring White Wolf and Soda Springs in Tuolumne Meadows into the park.

But the biggest battle between the private and the public interests would take place in the Hetch Hetchy Valley. It could be argued that the battle over damming the Tuolumne River within the boundaries of the fledgling park pitted one public entity (the national park) against another (the city of San Francisco), but the result was the same as selling off a parcel to a private interest. San Francisco was permitted to carve out and flood an entire valley within the public domain as a reservoir specifically for its own use. To this day, visitors can walk the shoreline in Hetch Hetchy, but the lake and the property that underlies it are off limits.

Many historians attribute the formation of the National Park Service to the Hetch Hetchy dam battle. The appropriation of such a huge swath of one of America's national parks spotlighted the need for an agency charged solely with their protection for the public benefit. Passage of the National Park Service Organic Act in 1916 created the National Park Service, which was charged with the promotion and regulation of the use of "national parks, monuments and reservations by such means and measures as conform to the fundamental purpose of the said parks, monuments and reservations, which purpose is to conserve the scenery and the natural and historic objects and the wild life therein and to provide for the enjoyment of the same in such manner and by such means as will leave them unimpaired for the enjoyment of future generations."

The creation of National Park Service represented a momentous shift in the evolution of preservation and conservation ethics on public lands across the United States. While the boundaries of Yosemite National Park remain fluid into modern times, the focus of redrawing the lines has become inclusive, with the goal of enhancing the Organic Act's charge.

THE CUTTING EDGE OF A REVOLUTIONARY IDEA

The tourists we saw were in parties of from three or four to fifteen or twenty, mounted on mules or small mustang ponies. A strange show they made, winding single file through the solemn woods in gaudy

attire, scaring the wild creatures, and one might fancy that even the great pines would be disturbed and groan aghast.
          —JOHN MUIR FROM *MY FIRST SUMMER IN THE SIERRA*

Despite his immediate recognition that Yosemite National Park would become a tourist mecca, John Muir could not have envisioned the growth in visitation that occurred in the following decades. Then again, no one could have. In the 1950s and 1960s, tourism grew by the tens of thousands

Visitors set up camp wherever they please in Stoneman Meadow. PHOTO TAKEN IN 1927, PHOTOGRAPHER UNKNOWN. COURTESY OF THE YOSEMITE NATIONAL PARK ARCHIVES, MUSEUM, AND LIBRARY.

each year. By the 1970s, summer seasons in Yosemite Valley were unadulterated craziness, with trailers parked side by side between the trees, meadows trampled, trails converted into human highways. The impacts were felt farther afield as well, most vividly illustrated in pictures showing the narrow ladder to the summit of Half Dome clotted with crowds. The wilderness that Muir had wandered through, and that Galen Clark had done his best to protect as Yosemite's guardian, was gone.

But accommodating tourism is one of the National Park Service's primary missions, and the agency has been extremely successful on that front. Consider the numbers. In 1906, the year Yosemite essentially took on its present configuration, about 5,500 people visited the park. By 1925, that number approached 210,000. In 1927, after the opening of the All-Year Highway linking Mariposa to El Portal and the Valley via the Merced River gorge, visitation topped 490,000. The numbers stayed flat through the 1930s and 1940s, when such extravagances as vacations were curtailed by the Great Depression and World War II. In the 1950s tourism spiked, with numbers topping one million through the latter part of the decade. A million-plus visitors in 1960 became two million-plus in 1970; the number topped three million for the first time in 1987, and broke through the four-million mark in 1996, where they've hovered ever since.

The trick has been coupling the success of visitation with the second prong of the park service mandate, which is to preserve the park's natural values. More people means more conflict and impact. Problem bears, insufficient parking, bogged traffic, and a lack of accommodations have all made headlines over the years, with Yosemite's managers scrambling to come up with strategies that would accommodate the crowds without thrashing the natural wonders that drew them together.

Yosemite was the first of its kind, and in melding the two park service missions, it would engineer more firsts. For many years the answers were more reactive than proactive. When car campers took to setting up tents anywhere they pleased in meadows on the Valley floor, the park established campgrounds to contain the damage. When begging bears became an issue, the park's initial responses ended up being disastrous for the bruins, but as time went on, rangers and administrators partnered with

Ranger-naturalist Enid Michael and one of Yosemite's black bears.
NATIONAL PARK SERVICE HISTORIC PHOTOGRAPH COLLECTION, COURTESY SHIRLEY SARGENT

wildlife biologists to figure out how best to both preserve the animals and mitigate impacts on visitors. On the proactive side, the National Park Service's first director, Stephen Mather, promoted winter development in Yosemite, the idea being to transform the park into a year-round playground. Badger Pass was developed as a result, and Yosemite's wintertime visitation increased dramatically.

Administratively, Yosemite hired the first "commissioned" female ranger in the National Park Service, Clare Marie Hodges, who worked a mounted patrol beginning in 1918. Enid Michael is recognized as the park service's first female ranger-naturalist. Michael, an accomplished mountaineer, was also a botanist, and dedicated much of her work in the Valley to maintaining its natural wildflower displays and cultivating a wildflower garden for educational purposes.

While the relationship hasn't been an easy one, the park worked with its renegade and inventive community of rock climbers to manage the extreme sports that flourished on the Valley's big walls. Yosemite Search and Rescue (YOSAR), called "one of the most well-oiled SAR machines in the world" by *Climbing* magazine, was a pioneer in recruiting big-wall climbers to assist in rescues, and in developing helicopter rescue techniques.

Though not the only park to do so, Yosemite embraced the New Deal. There is hardly a man-made improvement in the park that doesn't bear the mark of the Civilian Conservation Corps (CCC). This program brought ingenuity and exceptional workmanship to construction projects throughout the park in the 1930s. The young men of the Corps—more than six thousand occupied ten camps in Yosemite between 1933 and 1942, according to a 2005 profile by the Yosemite Association—did everything from rehabbing James Lamon's apple orchard to building the Arch Rock entrance and a ranger residence at Badger Pass. The corpsmen also constructed overlooks on Glacier Point and elsewhere; configured paths in the Mariposa Grove of Big Trees; built or rehabilitated trails in both the Valley and the backcountry; and improved campgrounds.

The park also embraced a first-of-its-kind partnership with the Yosemite Museum Association (now the Yosemite Conservancy) in 1923. This ongoing collaboration augments sometimes sketchy government allocations, supporting cultural and historic assets, habitat restoration, research, trail repair, visitor services, and wildlife management. The public-private collaboration also birthed the Yosemite Museum—another first—in 1926. The museum now has millions of items in its collections, from historic photos to Indian basketry to geologic and animal specimens. The associated Yosemite Archives contain millions of documents and records. This partnership has become a model for local, state, and national parks around the country. At the Presidio of San Francisco, a national park with close ties to Yosemite, a public-private partnership, the Presidio Trust, has allowed that park to endure as a self-sustaining entity; without it, the park service would not have been able to preserve the site.

On the educational front, Yosemite's interpretive programs got their start in 1920. *Yosemite Nature Notes*, chronicling the natural and human history of the park, were first published in 1922, and continue into modern times online and as a video series. In 1925 the Yosemite Field School of Natural History began training budding naturalists; this too continues into modern times as Outdoor Adventures.

Broader governmental and National Park Services initiatives, from park-wide general plans to sweeping NPS programs like Mission 66—which provided funding for physical improvements of park infrastructure, including controversial improvements to the Tioga Road in the park's high country—have shaped Yosemite in modern times. Significantly, the 1964 Wilderness Act and the 1984 California Wilderness Act enabled irrefutable protections for Yosemite's backcountry resources; 95 percent of the park is now designated wilderness, including the land above the waterline in Hetch Hetchy. Conservation is at play, but in times of increased environmental pressure, preservation has come to the fore.

INALIENABLE FOR ALL TIME

In setting Yosemite aside as a national preserve and playground, a nation emerging from civil war created something novel. The impetus may have been as simple and pure as the desire to do something creative in a destructive time. People were in mourning for lost sons, brothers, and fathers; the landscapes that had nurtured them for a hundred years were scorched and blood-soaked. But there, in the new state of California, was a place that didn't know war, that hadn't been ravaged, that was pristine. With the Yosemite Grant, the nation ensured that place would be preserved. In establishing the national parks that followed in Yosemite's broad wake, America made certain that other exceptional landscapes would also be thus protected.

The concept is clear, but the execution was, and remains, an evolutionary process. The ideas of preservation and conservation may have the same wellspring, but what they mean in practice—especially in as complex a proposition as a national park—has proven, at times, brilliant, provocative, and controversial.

The tests are unending. As this book went to press, the park was tackling yet another evolutionary issue, one Olmsted, Muir, and Clark could not have envisioned. Delaware North, which managed Yosemite's concessions for more than twenty years, acquired trademarks on the names of iconic structures including the Ahwahnee Hotel, Curry Village, and Badger Pass, as well as on the phrase "Yosemite National Park." At issue is money: The value of such names is difficult to peg, and the question of whether the trademarks should have been granted in the first place is also on the table. Remedies were being sought through the courts and the US Patent and Trademark Office as of spring 2016, but pending resolution, the Ahwahnee was renamed The Majestic Yosemite Hotel, Curry Village was dubbed Half Dome Village, and the Badger Pass Ski Area became the Yosemite Ski & Snowboard Area. The park has revised its concession contract to ensure that, going forward, concessionaires won't be able to trademark landmark names, and the hope is that these name changes are temporary.

It's impossible to know what the next challenge will be. Yosemite is the crucible—from a policy standpoint, it will likely remain forever a work in progress. But some things will outlast all political and commercial assaults. The machinations of humans can't touch El Capitan, Yosemite Falls, or Tuolumne Meadows, the very things that make Yosemite, first and foremost, America's flagship national park.

Building an Icon:
Yosemite's Roads, Trails, and Lodgings

From the moment American pioneers set eyes on the Yosemite Valley, they knew it was too big and too beautiful to keep secret. The problem: It was inherently inhospitable. It was vertical granite and breath-stealing altitude and wicked weather and wild animals.

No matter; these men and women knew Yosemite was the next big thing. They knew, once the word got out, that everyone would want to see it. They would *pay* to see it.

The challenge was getting tourists into the Valley quickly and safely. After all, Yosemite was miles from anywhere. And because this was no day trip, visitors would need a place to stay, and things to do aside from gawk at the waterfalls and mountaintops from the Valley floor. They'd need ways to explore, paths to take them to the falls and into the canyons and onto the summits with some measure of ease.

Building Yosemite involved trial and error, feats of engineering, elbow grease, and explosives. Only the fittest survived, as the park's roads, trails, hotels, and camps negotiated an ongoing balancing act of desire versus necessity. Those facilities that have withstood the test of time require diligent and ongoing maintenance, involving more elbow grease and clever engineering, with an eye toward the wallops that nature will hurl at them.

This is the story of how the inhospitable was made hospitable.

On the Roads
First things first. Yosemite's earliest promoters knew that if the Valley were to become a premier destination, people needed to get there.

Following Indian trails and bushwhacking had worked for trappers and prospectors, but tourists needed something more civilized.

Not that the old Indian trails weren't of use. The ancient routes linking tribe to tribe and summer camp to winter camp provided the sound, if rough, foundations for roads and trails still being used in Yosemite National Park today. The terrain dictated the way, and the Miwok and Mono Paiute had laid the tracks. Their footpaths only had to be improved.

The first Indian trail to be converted into a tourist route traveled up from the frontier outpost of Mariposa to what would become Wawona, and then down into Yosemite Valley. The Mann brothers, Milton and Houston, established an arduous but passable "toll road," essentially a horse trail, along that route in the mid-1850s. It took a couple of days to make the passage, which climbed Chowchilla Mountain, wound through the woodlands south of the Valley's rim, then dove via steep grades and switchbacks to the Valley floor near the base of Bridalveil Fall. Only a handful of people took on the challenge, and no one made the journey in winter.

The Mann toll road, which opened in 1856, was followed on quickly by a pair of trails that dropped into the Valley from the north side—neither of which, apparently, followed old Indian routes. The Coulterville Free Road climbed to the north rim via Bower's Cave, then passed north of the Merced Grove and crossed Tamarack and Crane Flats before careening down to the Valley floor near the base of El Capitan. The Big Oak Flat Trail started in the town of the same name, traveled through Groveland, Buck Meadows, and Harden Flat (all of which lie along present-day CA 120), met the Coulterville Road at Crane Flat, and then proceeded to the Valley floor via that route.

Little more than a hundred visitors traveled to the Valley annually in those early years. And that wasn't just because the routes into the Valley itself were so strenuous. To get to Yosemite from any major city involved days of travel by boat, stage, and later, train, and was typically undertaken only by the elite, who had the time and money to make the trip. Take, for example, the journey from San Francisco, one of the most popular points of departure. From the Bay Area, travelers sailed or steamed up the San Joaquin River to the town of Stockton. There they picked up a

Steep switchbacks enabled wagon travel from the north rim to the Valley floor.
PHOTO: J. T. BOYSEN, 1903. COURTESY OF THE YOSEMITE NATIONAL PARK ARCHIVES, MUSEUM, AND LIBRARY.

stagecoach that rumbled down rough roads through the Central Valley to Mariposa or Coulterville, where they loaded themselves and their luggage onto horseback in "saddle trains" for the arduous final leg.

In the 1870s, with the approval of the Yosemite Grant's board of commissioners, the horse trails were "improved" as wagon roads. Two turnpike companies engaged in a race to the Valley floor on the north side, and the Wawona Road, on the south side, proceeded as well. Some realignment was required: The Coulterville Road, which opened in 1874 as a partial toll road, was rerouted through the Merced Grove and present-day Foresta before taking the plunge into the Merced River gorge and landing near The Cascades. The Big Oak Flat wagon road was finished a month later: This was rerouted near the Tuolumne Grove before making a steep descent into the Valley. The grades were ominous. One history reports an average grade of 8 percent, with some sections sharpening to 16 percent, and the roadway was only thirteen feet wide. The Wawona Road, covering twenty-seven miles and including a covered bridge over the south fork of the Merced, was finished in 1875. The Grand Carriage Drive on the Valley floor, started in 1880, integrated both new construction and portions of existing roads that were purchased under the auspices of the Yosemite Grant Act. Modern access to the park, on CA 120 (the Big Oak Flat Road), CA 41 (the Wawona Road), and Northside and Southside Drives, follow the alignments of these pioneer routes, at least in part.

The ancestral Mono Trail, which links Yosemite to the Mono Lake basin on the east side of the Sierra, underlays what is now the spectacular Tioga Road. Winding along the divide between the Merced and Tuolumne drainages, the old Indian thruway was used by Lieutenant Tredwell Moore and his men to pursue a group of Yosemite Indians who had killed prospectors in the Valley in 1852, and also by John Muir during his explorations as a sheepherder in his first summer in the Sierra. The trail over Tioga Pass later allowed access to high-country mining camps in what was known as the Tioga silver district. The Golden Crown Mine, the Grand Sierra, and other claims on the "mother lode of the Great Silver Belt" were short-lived, as was the mining camp at Bennettsville, but the Great Sierra Wagon Road, built using pickaxes and powder in the early 1880s by crews fortified with Chinese immigrants, was etched into the wilderness to serve them.

Given the radical conditions at altitude—Tioga Pass tops out at nearly ten thousand feet—and the lack of maintenance following the abandonment of the mines, the condition of the wagon road quickly deteriorated. But it remained in use and, given the quality of its alignment through difficult topography, was considered a valuable asset. In 1915 Stephen Mather, who would become the first chief of the National Park Service, spearheaded rehabilitation of the former toll road, and then orchestrated its purchase, funded in part with his own money, and subsequent donation to Yosemite National Park.

Driving over the road in newfangled automobiles quickly gained popularity, despite the ongoing battle against weather and erosion. One section was paved in 1937, which allowed easier access to the spectacular sights along the route in the summertime. Further improvements and realignments were made in the late 1950s and early 1960s, but these were controversial, with the Sierra Club and photographer Ansel Adams deploring the construction techniques employed, particularly the blasting of polished granite alongside Tenaya Lake. But despite the improvements, alpine conditions force closure of the road each winter, as snow piles deep and chips away at Tioga's integrity.

Providing winter access to Yosemite Valley was a priority in the 1920s, both for park officials and concessionaires. The El Portal Road (CA 140), the park's "all-weather highway," was completed in 1926, and followed the alignment of the wagon road used to help build the Yosemite Valley Railroad, which was completed in 1907. Linking the Valley to Mariposa, the El Portal Road's low elevation and modest grade, following the relatively gentle pitch of the Merced River, made traveling to the park easy for motorists and tour buses. Following completion of the Wawona Tunnel in 1933, the Wawona Road was plowed through the winter, allowing access to the Valley from the south, and permitting travelers to reach the Glacier Point Road and the ski area at Badger Pass.

Once the major roadways were in place, their maintenance and improvement became the focus. Before the National Park Service was established in 1916, the US Army troops patrolled the roads outside the Yosemite Grant and undertook their care and maintenance. The 1930s were productive in terms of repair and revitalization, with the young men of the Civilian Conservation Corps (CCC) repaving and augmenting many of the park's highways. The tunnels and overlooks on Big Oak Flat Road (CA 120), which offers a stunning introduction to Yosemite Valley from the north, were constructed in this decade, along with the famous Tunnel View overlook on the Wawona Road.

The advent of the automobile age forever altered Yosemite National Park. For the park's first quarter-century or so, with access mostly via horseback, an average of twelve thousand people toured Yosemite Valley each year. That began to change in 1900, when photographer Oliver Lippincott motored into the Valley in his Locomobile, the first car to enter the park and, by one account, the first to enter any national park.

In the next few years a smattering of autos made the long, engine-cooking journey to the Valley via the Wawona Road, along with a motorcycle or two. But vehicles weren't welcome. The park's acting superintendent, Major H. C. Benson, banned cars from the Valley in 1907, maintaining that the grades on the wagon roads were too steep, and fearing snarls with stages. The ban wouldn't last, as technical advancements made motor vehicles more viable on mountain roads, and as cars grew more popular with the public. Automobiles were becoming a permanent fixture—one that even an aging John Muir recognized as a force to be accommodated rather than shunned. The ban was overturned by the secretary of the interior in 1913.

Still, for another few years, auto traffic into the Valley was relatively light. By one count about 200 cars entered the park via the Wawona Road in 1912, albeit without legal authorization. In 1915, author Keith Trexler notes, "190 cars entered the park via Tioga Pass, and the following year 578 westbound autos checked in at Tuolumne Meadows." The numbers are piddling by today's standards, but that trickle would become a flood by the end of the century, with thousands of cars clogging the asphalt tracks on the Valley floor and jamming the access roads each summer season.

Northside and Southside Roads, which form a loop on the Valley floor, have been in place for more than a century, but the boom in visitation in the mid-twentieth century resulted in aggravating traffic jams in the heart of the park. In the 1970s the loop was converted to a one-way system, accommodating two lanes of traffic, and a shuttle service was established. The Valley floor is still congested in high season, but at least now the traffic moves.

While managing the seasonal hordes within the Valley and on the more than two hundred miles of paved roadway in Yosemite National Park remains a challenge, the park is nonetheless accessible year-round, and that's a feat its pioneer entrepreneurs would have relished.

The Trails

Cables on a cliff face. Sixty switchbacks in a mile. A staircase so close to a waterfall that the stonework is never free of mist. Yosemite's trails are a marvel of design and engineering, and the builders are, in the estimation of generations of hikers, geniuses. Daring and farsighted trailblazers like John Conway surveyed sometimes devious, always brilliant lines to the tops of waterfalls, around Glacier Point, through the woodlands of Wawona, into the remote canyons of the Tuolumne, and onto the highest peaks along the Sierra Crest. Their work opened the park to both day hiker and long-distance wanderer.

Conway is one of a cadre of talented trail builders who chiseled paths onto Yosemite's walls and into the backcountry. The park's first hikers were bushwhackers, men like John Muir and Galen Clark and Clarence King, who used Indian and game trails where they could find them, but had the skill and sense to travel safely cross-country and then find their way home again.

But not all of Yosemite's visitors have been born with, or care to cultivate, a sense of how to walk in the woods. Even with trails some get themselves into trouble, overestimating their physical strength, the grip of their footwear, or their ability to withstand heat and cold and altitude.

A trail builder can only do so much to ameliorate those failings. A seasoned hiker may contemplate with dread the prospect of ascending three thousand feet in four miles, but at least there's a notion of what the endeavor requires. And that seasoned hiker is the one who will truly appreciate what Yosemite's trail builders have created: paths that, if taken at the right pace and in the right time, are among the best in the world.

Conway, dubbed "the master trail-builder of the Valley" by John Muir, configured several iconic trails in the park. Climbing from floor to rim is a wicked endeavor no matter how it's executed, but Conway's quick switchbacks are surprisingly easy on the knees and lungs. He is the architect of the trails that ascend alongside Yosemite Falls (built in the 1870s; the trail of sixty switchbacks) and Chilnualna Falls near Wawona. Equally cunning is the Four Mile Trail (also built in the early 1870s), which starts at the base of Sentinel Rock and climbs to Glacier Point. Helen Hunt Jackson, author of *Ramona* (1884), is quoted as calling this "a marvelous piece of work. It is broad, smooth, and well protected on the outer edge, in all dangerous places, by large rocks; so that, although it is [by] far the steepest trail out of the Valley, zigzagging back and forth on a sheer granite wall, one rides up it with little alarm or giddiness, and with such a sense of gratitude to the builder that the dollar's toll seems too small."

Many of Yosemite's iconic pathways were initially toll trails, and were purchased from the trail builders once the Yosemite Grant was established. The Mist Trail, in particular, has an interesting toll-trail history. Before the heralded stone steps were built into the cliff alongside Vernal Fall, a series of ladders assisted in the ascent, and, like the steps, were constantly inundated with water. Historians quote one nineteenth-century hiker as saying, "There is an awfully pokerish ladder fastened against the cliff on which you can go down and get very wet. It is painful and rather dangerous, but a great many persons escape, and they only charge you seventy-five cents." The ladders were replaced by wooden steps after the death of a hiker, and at the turn of the twentieth century, by the stone staircase in place today.

Conway is also remembered for blazing a trail into Little Yosemite Valley and installing the first bolts on the lower reaches of the famous final pitch up the smooth granite of Half Dome. Although Conway's crew retreated before reaching the summit, the route he started would be incorporated into Half Dome's first ascent, made in 1875 by George Anderson. Since then, the trail to the summit of the dome has been a bucket-list hike for visitors to Yosemite. That final pitch might well be described as an aid climb, most definitely not to be undertaken by the faint of heart, knee, or nerve. The cables and footrests on the sloping face of the dome today, originally installed by the Sierra Club in 1919 and rebuilt and reinforced by the CCC in the 1930s, provide the only safe way for hikers to reach the summit.

Yosemite hikers also tread softly on the work of Gabriel Sovulewski. A native of Poland, he emigrated to the United States as a teenager and found work, initially, in Chicago, then opted to join the US Army. As described by his granddaughter, Charlotte Ewing, in an oral history, the future supervisor of Yosemite National Park was a proponent of leaving no trace long before it became a slogan, teaching her and visitors to the park how to "treat the land, to take care of it, and to leave it for other people."

Before the stone steps were built, the trail alongside Vernal Fall included a wooden ladder. PHOTO: GEORGE FISKE; FROM THE 1880S. COURTESY OF THE YOSEMITE NATIONAL PARK ARCHIVES, MUSEUM, AND LIBRARY.

Park supervisor and trail builder Gabriel Sovulewski in 1896. PHOTO: E. GOODRICH. COURTESY OF THE YOSEMITE NATIONAL PARK ARCHIVES, MUSEUM, AND LIBRARY.

Sovulewski was assigned to Camp A. E. Wood in Wawona in 1893, a member of one of the US Army units that patrolled the newly established park. He spent three years in Yosemite before being transferred to serve in the Philippines, and returned following the 1906 earthquake as the park's supervisor, a position that became, in one form or another, permanent. He, like Galen Clark and John Muir, with whom he was acquainted, became a Yosemite devotee. How could he not? The front porch of his home in the Valley, his granddaughter recalled, had a view of Glacier Point, and the back porch looked out on Yosemite Falls.

Yosemite's trails were Sovulewski's passion, and remain his legacy. He is credited with transforming game trails and the bare-bones tracks established by Indians—the most logical lines through Yosemite's canyons and into its wildlands—into today's functional routes. He cleared the treadways and blazed them so they could be easily followed, etching diamonds onto trees to keep trekkers on course. He is credited with composing this list of what a trail builder must possess to succeed in the endeavor: "strength, determination, a natural instinct for direction, love for the work, love of nature, and an ability to forget everything for the time except the object in view, and to be able to sit in the saddle for 12 or

14 hours, or walk the same number of hours if required in order to find the best possible way."

Not all trails in Yosemite were a success, however. Case in point: the Ledge Trail, which climbed LeConte Gully from the Valley floor to Glacier Point. Established in the 1870s, the trail, which gained three thousand feet in two miles, proved so steep and hazardous that people could, and did, just walk right off the edge, plunging thousands of feet to their deaths. To stem the carnage, the park prohibited downhill travel on the route in 1928, but when that failed—young men, in particular, had a propensity for disregarding even the most blatant warnings—in 1958 the trail was removed from park maps and abandoned altogether.

Yosemite's eight hundred miles of trail, like its roads, require ongoing care and maintenance. But unlike roadwork, trail work in the park involves grit, strength, and the patience of a puzzle master. The techniques used today are those of the pioneers, who incorporated what they found on the ground to delineate and shore up treadways. The CCC became masters of this kind of masonry, which involves no mortar, no hydraulics, no blasting. Just "hug, lean, and roll," then stop, survey, and do it again.

But a palpable contentedness permeates the work. Whether laboring high in the backcountry, levering blocks of granite, or behind Yosemite Village, meticulously and thoughtfully tapping stones in place on a short staircase leading to the paved Valley Loop, trail workers exude joy. They, like Sovulewski, know that what they create and maintain complements and renders accessible one of the greatest landscapes on Earth.

PLACES TO STAY

The contrast is striking. There's the Ahwahnee Hotel, a national historic landmark dating back to 1927, massive and stately, warm and elegantly rustic, great windows opening onto storied vistas and sunlight that fires up the sparkle in the champagne. Then there's the pup tent, sagging between two pitchy pines within yards of the busy loop road, humble and avoided until the last ember of the campfire fizzles, then not abandoned until sunshine burns off the morning chill and the air outside is warmer than the inside of the sleeping bag.

Yosemite's long-lived Sentinel Hotel. COURTESY OF THE YOSEMITE NATIONAL PARK
ARCHIVES, MUSEUM, AND LIBRARY

In Yosemite's early days, the tent, or its rawboned wooden equivalent, was all a traveler could hope to find for lodging in the Valley—or anywhere near the Valley, for that matter. But the innkeepers kept coming; they knew the park was a different kind of California gold mine, and providing a room was one way to cash in.

Within a few years of its "discovery" by the Mariposa Battalion in 1851, James Hutchings, a gold miner turned publisher, toured Yosemite Valley and deemed it a "wonderful, mountain-bound valley of waterfalls." He quickly calculated its potential as a tourist attraction and set about promoting it in his publication, *Hutchings' Illustrated California Magazine.* Artist Thomas Ayres was hired to illustrate the falls and domes for the magazine, but the artist found the task challenging given the scale of the landscape. Likewise, while readers across the country were enchanted by the descriptions in Hutchings's articles, they were challenged by the notion that such a mammoth place could actually exist.

But Hutchings proved a skilled marketer, and by the end of the decade the sightseers, the searchers, and the entrepreneurs began to filter into Yosemite. Some would come and go, but others longed to stay, and devised ways to make a living off the beautiful but difficult land. One of those searchers, Galen Clark, found health, peace, and a lifelong mission as guardian of the Yosemite Grant, but he began by establishing a way station on the long road through Wawona. James Lamon, who arrived in the late 1850s, homesteaded in the Valley, planting orchards and other crops to see him through the long winters, the first few of which he endured alone. He would remain in the Valley until his death in 1875, and is interred in the Yosemite Cemetery.

To satisfy his Yosemite yearnings, Hutchings became one of a long list of innkeepers who built and ran hotels and camps in the Yosemite Valley. The first "hotel" was erected in 1856 at the foot of Sentinel Rock. Known as the Lower Hotel, it was managed in those earliest years by the Neals; wife Jean was one of the first white women to see Yosemite Valley, according to one historian. The Hite "canvas house" was built in 1858, and the wood-frame Upper Hotel in 1859. Hutchings purchased the Upper Hotel in 1864, renamed it the Hutchings House, and brought his wife, Elvira, and mother-in-law to the Valley to help him run the business. In addition to entertaining visitors, Hutchings and Elvira started a family in Yosemite. Their daughter, Florence, was the first white child born in the park, and the couple also raised William and Gertrude, known as "Cosie," in the Valley.

The passage of the Yosemite Grant Act changed the nature of business in the Valley. The government set about buying back private inholdings like those held by Hutchings, Lamon, and others, and imposed ten-year leases on properties within the Yosemite Grant's boundaries. Though he battled the enforcement of eminent domain in the state legislature and the courts, Hutchings would eventually be forced out, and his hotel would fall to the care of a different manager, and then another. The provisions of the Yosemite Grant translated, in many instances, to quick turnover of management. The names of the hotels and their proprietors changed in those decades with bewildering frequency, some lasting the full ten years, others selling out, still others just walking away. Later, after the National

Park Service was established, leases for lodging and services would be held by concessionaires, and these companies—the Desmond, the Curry, and others—would shape the nature of business in Yosemite into modern times.

Though state and federal supervision would eventually reconfigure and consolidate what private interests established on the Valley floor, Yosemite hosted two distinct villages in the late nineteenth century—the Lower (or Old) Village and the Upper Village, connected by a boardwalk. Lodges were the backbones of the two commercial hubs. Black's Hotel was open for business, as was the Leidig Hotel, known for the scrumptious meals prepared by Belle Leidig. The Sentinel Hotel, once the Hutchings House, boasted its remarkable Big Tree Room, built around a huge incense cedar. The Stoneman House was California's first attempt to provide upscale and consistent accommodations on the Valley floor, in contrast to the sometimes chaotic management of the other hotels. Completed in 1887, the grand hotel boasted three floors and a gabled attic, with nearly seventy rooms for tourists. Plagued by structural inadequacies

The Stoneman House, the state of California's attempt to provide upscale accommodations for Yosemite visitors in the late nineteenth century, lasted about ten years before burning down. COURTESY OF THE YOSEMITE NATIONAL PARK ARCHIVES, MUSEUM, AND LIBRARY

necessitating constant attention, the Stoneman nonetheless fit the bill while it stood.

The Valley's villages encompassed more than just hotels and camps for tourists. The Cosmopolitan, a saloon and bathhouse outfitted with a separate parlor for ladies and a reading room for the gentlemen, along with a barbershop and boot-black stand, and entertainments including billiards, shuffleboard, and a shooting gallery, opened in 1870. Maps from the late 1800s and early 1900s show a woodworking shop, a blacksmith shop, a laundry, a schoolhouse, a dairy, Degnan's bakery, grocery and dry goods stores, a butcher shop, a sawmill, a hatchery, a Wells Fargo office, studios for landscape artists and photographers, a building for dynamite storage, stables, an elk paddock, a zoo, a separate village for the Indians who remained in the park, camps for cavalry units, employee housing, and more. The Village Chapel was open "for the free use of Christians of every denomination," as described by Hutchings in his lengthy book on Yosemite, *In the Heart of the Sierras.* The structures lined the narrow streets as in any frontier town.

Farther afield, Albert and Emily Snow opened La Casa Nevada, a popular "mountain chalet" on the flat step between Vernal and Nevada Falls. One historian quotes a friend of Emily Snow's who observed that the proprietress, while an engaging and competent hostess, was "always stewed to the eyeballs." Soused or not, Mrs. Snow is quoted by another historian as noting that the location of La Casa Nevada was "as close to heaven as you could get."

Meanwhile, on the south rim, James McCauley took over the "shanty" that had been erected on Glacier Point by Charles Peregoy, and replaced it with his Mountain House. Accessible at first only by the Four-Mile toll trail, when the Glacier Point Road (another masterpiece from the mind and hand of trail builder John Conway) was finished in 1882, the Mountain House became a sought-after destination. It was also home to Yosemite's famed Firefall, an artificial "waterfall" of embers that delighted tourists on summer nights for nearly a century.

Up at Wawona, known as Clark's Station in the early days, travelers seeking respite from the long, rough road, as well as those seeking to explore the Mariposa Grove of Big Trees, found hospitality at Galen

Clark's cabin, and, for a time, at a "public house" built and run by Charles Peregoy and his wife. By 1879 the impressive Wawona Hotel had been established by the Washburn family, and the brothers Washburn were well on their way to creating a thriving resort that endures into modern times.

In 1899, David Curry and his wife, Jennie, established a tent camp at the base of Glacier Point. This operation, which provided relatively low-cost accommodations to tourists, would grow into one of the most well-known, sprawling, and at times controversial, concessions within Yosemite Valley. The entrepreneurial vision and persistence of David Curry were core to the enterprise's long-lived success, but the ideal setting was also key. Camp Curry was located below the soaring face that hosted the popular Firefall, alongside Stoneman Meadow, with its stunning views of Half Dome, and near the meandering Merced. Despite conflicts with park managers, political disagreements, bureaucratic snarls, and the persistent chipping away at the number of tents and cabins in the camp—this accomplished, occasionally in spectacular fashion, by the threat of rockfall—Camp Curry, now Curry Village, remains one of the most popular destinations on the Valley floor.

Other commercial tent camps also blossomed in the Valley, including Camp Ahwahnee, which boasted a dining room and electric lighting, and Camp Lost Arrow. Both would be incorporated, along with the Sentinel Hotel, into what is now known as the Yosemite Lodge by a Curry Company competitor, the Desmond Park Service Company. The Desmond Company would also establish and operate the High Sierra Camps at Tenaya Lake, Tuolumne Meadows, Merced Lake, and elsewhere in the park's backcountry in the 1910s. The camps, according to park service literature, form a "High Sierra loop trail camp system designed to provide visitors with a backcountry experience while at the same time exposing them to wilderness values."

Gabriel Sovulewski established a series of public campgrounds around the Valley as well, numbered one through twenty (with no "thirteen," as that was considered unlucky). These would eventually be consolidated into the four campgrounds on the floor today.

Finding a balance between development of services for visitors and the maintenance of Yosemite's natural values has, since the establishment of the park, translated into the thoughtful whittling away at the number of accommodations provided, especially on the Valley floor. To accomplish this, in the early twentieth century, the park service slowly and methodically dismantled the Old Village on the south side of the Merced. Crews with the CCC helped "naturalize" the village site, and relocate or reconstruct the necessary infrastructure in the new Yosemite Village on the other side of the river. A few Old Village relics remain on the south side, including the Village Chapel and the LeConte Memorial Lodge.

Fire, rockfall, and flood have helped reduce development as well. Fire had long been the bane of the park's early hotels. Leidig's burned down in the early 1890s; a stand of locust trees marks the site. The Cosmopolitan building (by then no longer a saloon) was destroyed by fire in 1932. The Stoneman House burned in 1896. The Mountain House and the Glacier Point Hotel, a grand structure erected next door in the 1910s by the Desmond Company, were erased by flames in 1969. None have been replaced. Nearly three hundred units—tents and structures—in Curry Village were removed from circulation following a rockfall in 2008. The hundred-year flood on the Merced River in 1997 wiped out about four hundred campsites, and they haven't been reclaimed.

A WINTER WONDERLAND

Opening Yosemite to winter recreation proved transformative for the park. The Curry Company was an early promoter of snow sports, establishing a sledding hill called "Ash Can Alley" at its camp, and flooding the parking area to turn it into an ice rink. Mary Curry Tresidder, daughter of David and Jennie Curry, and her husband, Donald, who would serve as president of the Yosemite Park and Curry Company from 1927 to 1943, were both skiers and skaters, and promoted development of ski-touring facilities in the park. Mary Tresidder envisioned "Yosemite with its back-drop of beauty as an outstanding winter place," and predicted that "within a few years the High Sierra Camps would be a series of winter huts like those in the Alps, with skiers touring from one to another."

Yosemite's promise as a winter mecca even prompted a bid for the 1932 Winter Olympic Games. Though this failed to materialize—Lake

The Badger Pass Ski Area was built to help bring tourists
into Yosemite year-round. PHOTO: R. H. ANDERSON, 1936.
COURTESY OF THE YOSEMITE NATIONAL PARK ARCHIVES, MUSEUM,
AND LIBRARY.

Placid, New York, would host the games that year—the effort boosted
the park's public exposure. Yosemite also began hosting winter carnivals,
which would draw "an estimated 3,700 people" to Yosemite Valley in
1931, according to one historian. The Yosemite Winter Club got its start
in those years as well.

When their backcountry hut-to-hut ski enterprise failed to produce
great profits, the Tresidders set their sights on a downhill-skiing operation. Badger Pass was the result, one of the first downhill ski resorts in
California.

Recreation on the Badger Pass "ski fields" started in 1933; by 1935 the
ski lodge, the access road, ski runs, and an "up-ski," or tow, were installed.
Improvements in later years included a thirty-meter ski jump and the
addition of formal rope tows, T-bar lifts, and, finally, chairlifts. Located
off the Glacier Point Road at 8,500 feet, elements of the ski complex,
which covers nearly three hundred acres, were built by a CCC team in
1940. The Ostrander Ski Hut, linked to the ski area by a ten-mile backcountry trail, was erected by the CCC in a matter of months in 1941. And
the small ski hill was the site of the first National Ski Championships to
be held in California in 1942, "the only national ski competition to be

held during World War II," according to documentation advocating the resort's inclusion on the National Register of Historic Places.

The Tresidders were also a driving force behind the construction of the Ahwahnee, Yosemite's first year-round hotel. The contrast with Camp Curry couldn't have been more pronounced. The hotel, promoted by National Park Service chief Stephen Mather, who wanted to attract wealthy vacationers to the park, was designed by architect Gilbert Stanley

The Ahwahnee was, and remains, Yosemite's hotel of choice for the upper class. COURTESY OF THE YOSEMITE NATIONAL PARK ARCHIVES, MUSEUM, AND LIBRARY

Underwood and outfitted for upper-class patrons, with stunning views, fine dining rooms, posh suites, and pricing to match. Fittingly, the hotel is home the annual Bracebridge Dinner, an extravaganza of fine food and theater hearkening back to Yuletide feasts hosted by old English aristocracy.

Completed in 1927, the hotel struggled financially at first; Yosemite and all its concessions took a hit during the Great Depression. But in World War II, business at the hotel took an unexpected turn. As described in park literature, the hotel's managers were "undoubtedly looking for a temporary solution to the Ahwahnee's red ink woes when the Department of the Navy offered a long-term arrangement to rent the entire hotel." The Ahwahnee was commissioned as the "U.S. Naval Convalescent Hospital Yosemite National Park, California" in 1943. Though the setting couldn't have been more idyllic, the soldiers sent to convalesce there, whether from shell shock or physical injury, struggled with the seclusion. One staff member is quoted as saying, "If the patients weren't nuts when they got to Yosemite, the boredom there soon sent them over the edge."

To improve morale, additions were made to the hotel's amenities, including a library, a bowling alley, a pool hall, and "last but not least, building the servicemen's own 'Oasis' beer joint, the only authorized pub in any Naval hospital around the world." With the focus shifted from straight rehab to a more well-rounded approach to wellness, the Ahwahnee hospital experience was touted as "a watershed event in the development of US military medical rehabilitation techniques."

AT TRAILS' END

Despite losing his Yosemite Valley hotel in 1874, James Hutchings remained a tireless promoter of Yosemite and an enduring character in the park story. He employed a young, bewitched John Muir at his sawmill, but that relationship, the story goes, was troubled by jealousy, as Hutchings's wife, Elvira, favored the wandering naturalist, and because Muir's writings garnered more fame and prestige than Hutchings's did. He served as Yosemite guardian from 1880 to 1884, but the tenure was troubled and he was not asked to stay on. Yosemite's first marketer died in the Valley, in a buggy accident near the base of the Big Oak Flat Road in 1902, and he is buried in the Yosemite Cemetery.

The successes and travails of James Hutchings are emblematic of what all who would "develop" Yosemite National Park have endured for love of the place. They have dreamed and schemed and built up the park, only to see that their contributions could, in the end, be erased from the landscape by landslide or politics, fire or bureaucracy.

Yosemite the place carries on without them. Yosemite the place doesn't care if a tourist is comfortable. Can't find a parking place? Hotels all full? Twist your ankle on the trail? Yosemite the place remains impassive; this is *your* problem.

But Yosemite the park cares deeply. Yosemite the park paves and repaves, builds and rebuilds, razes and restores, all to ensure that visitors are safe and comfortable. For better or for worse, the park conforms to the contours, listens to the needs, juggles the curveballs thrown by nature, politics, and business. Yosemite the park abides within what Yosemite the place allows.

The Quiet Giants:
Galen Clark and the Big Trees

A SICK MAN WANDERED INTO THE DEEP WOODS SOUTH OF THE YOSEMITE Valley and settled there for a time. He'd seen the storied cliffs and waterfalls, but he chose the forest, and there he found well-being. He also found giant sequoias, trees as monumental as the falls and domes of the celebrated gorge a few steep miles distant. The trees and the man shared more than common ground, both possessing the steadiness and grace to thrive within the spotlight but with a foot outside, rooted in peace and quiet.

Galen Clark's hand lies gently on much of what Yosemite is today. His name isn't as well known as some others associated with the park: Muir, Roosevelt, Lincoln, even James Hutchings. The mark of Yosemite's longtime guardian wasn't made by writing bestsellers or winning elections. He was a builder and a guide, one the park would turn to twice in its early years as it coped with growing pains.

Clark began his long Yosemite sojourn as a host in what would become known as Wawona. The resort that grew up there, in the meadows near the giant sequoia groves, has proven another steady, enduring, quiet star of the park. While other hotels came and went down on the Valley floor, victims of political wrangling and fire, the Wawona Hotel has remained open for business into modern times.

The giant sequoias endure as well, having survived thousands of years of fire, deluge, and drought, and the greed of humankind. They are not as old as the rock, but some are older than any other living thing on the planet, and more massive as well. Perhaps, in their way, the big trees conferred upon the man and the settlement the blessings of a long life, well lived.

The Big Trees

And I've been to the groves of Sequoia Big Trees,
  Where beauty and grandeur combine,
Grand Temples of Nature for worship and ease,
  Enchanting, inspiring, sublime!
—Prologue to Galen Clark's *The Big Trees of California*

California is a land of tree huggers, for better or for worse. There's a good chance, on any day, at any point in time, while walking through the Mariposa Grove or the Tuolumne Grove or the Merced Grove, you'll find someone pressed up against a massive trunk, hands flat on the cinnamon bark, attempting to give a big tree a squeeze. It looks ridiculous—and the tree couldn't care less—but the gesture of gratitude reflects the awe giant sequoias inspire.

It starts and ends with their size. To say the giant sequoia is the largest living organism on Earth doesn't begin to describe how monumental these trees are. They aren't as tall as their cousins, the coast redwoods, which can reach upward of 375 feet. The tallest sequoia reaches just more than 300 feet. But they dwarf the redwood in girth. Once Yosemite's biggest sequoia, the Washington Tree in the Mariposa Grove, which partially collapsed in 2005, measured more than 95 feet in circumference at the base; the General Sherman Tree in Sequoia & Kings Canyon National Park measures more than 102 feet around. The biggest coast redwoods, by comparison, only attain a svelte 70 feet on average.

The differences in dimension can be attributed to habitat, evolution, and life span. Giant sequoias are also the oldest living things on the planet, with some trees estimated to be more than three thousand years old. The oldest coast redwoods, by comparison, are at least a thousand years younger. Given that extra millennium, and a metabolism perfectly adapted to its environment, it's understandable that the giant sequoia, *Sequoiadendron giganteum*, would be able to pack on some impressive tonnage.

The sequoias extant today—in the Sierra, along northern California's coast, and in China, where the dawn redwood is found—are descended from much larger sequoia forests that stretched across the northern latitudes. The giant sequoias adapted as the Sierra rose, taking root at elevations where hardwoods, like oaks and maples, couldn't thrive. Climatic and geologic shifts forced the trees to specialize, much as diverse conditions forced adaptations among the coast and dawn redwoods.

Three groves of giant sequoias are protected within Yosemite National Park. The Mariposa Grove, part of the initial Yosemite Grant of 1864, lies about four miles southeast of Wawona. It was "discovered" in early summer 1857. The story goes that Galen Clark and Milton Mann, one of the Mann brothers who would later build the Wawona toll trail, found the grove while following the lead of a hunter who had reported seeing giant trees in the area. Mann would build a trail into the grove so that others could visit and wonder; Clark would set about documenting the heights, circumferences, locations, and other physical characteristics of the trees. The Tuolumne Grove, on the north side of the Yosemite Valley, was "discovered" in 1858, and the Merced Grove, while it may have been seen first by the Walker party in 1833, was put on the map when the Coulterville toll road was built. Dr. John McLean, who had the lease on the Coulterville concern, rerouted his road to run through the grove, adding a tourist attraction to the otherwise relatively onerous route.

The Grizzly Giant. PHOTO: CARLETON WATKINS. DIGITAL IMAGE COURTESY OF THE GETTY'S OPEN CONTENT PROGRAM.

The Mariposa Grove is actually two groves, the Upper containing more than 260 trees, and the Lower encompassing more than 240. The Grizzly Giant is the oldest and one of the most striking trees in the groves. The giant, standing just more than two hundred feet tall, has a diameter of more than twenty-seven feet at the base, and a prominent limb about a hundred feet off the ground that measures nearly twenty feet around. "The Grizzly Giant must be not less than six thousand years old," Clark wrote in *The Big Trees of California*, "yet still living, grizzled with age, defying old Time with his legions of furies which have shattered its royal crown, stripped its body nearly bare, and cut off its main source of nutriment. Dying for centuries, yet still standing at bay, it is probably not only the oldest living tree, but also the oldest living thing on earth." As it turns out, Clark vastly overestimated the Grizzly Giant's age, which modern literature pegs at about 2,700 years. For all that the estimate was halved, its life span is still extraordinary.

The Mariposa Grove contains other remarkable named trees as well, including the Fallen Monarch, a massive sequoia that, hundreds of years after death, holds its form due to tannins that preserve the wood and thick bark. William Brewer, traveling with a survey party led by California State Geologist Josiah Whitney in the early 1860s, also noted how extraordinarily resilient the wood was as he documented a sequoia that had recently been harvested. The tree, which took twenty-seven men four days to take down, was determined to be 1,255 years old. "It is remarkable that the wood should be sound that was already over eight hundred years old when Columbus set out on his voyage of discovery," Brewer wrote.

Then there are the tunnel trees, with openings carved in their bases to allow passage of carriages and stagecoaches—and later, automobiles—carrying sightseers. "These trees had been burned to such an extent that widening out the passage for stages did not injure the roots or vitality and cannot properly be termed an act of spoilation or vandalism," Clark observed. "A ride through these trees in a six-horse stage, or any conveyance, is a great novelty and should not be missed." The tunnel through what is now called the Fallen Wawona Tunnel Tree was carved in 1881. The tree toppled after record snows fell in 1969, and there is some

The Mariposa Grove's famous Wawona Tunnel Tree (now fallen). PHOTO: HENRY G. PEABODY. COURTESY OF THE NATIONAL PARK SERVICE HISTORIC PHOTOGRAPH COLLECTION.

speculation that cutting the tunnel did contribute to its demise. The California Tunnel Tree was cut in 1895; it still abides. And fire is, as Clark noted, responsible for naturally creating tunnels in giant sequoias. For example, fire has gutted the Telescope Tree from ground to crown, allowing a shaft of light to pierce the interior.

The Tuolumne Grove is located on the north rim near Crane Flat, off the Tioga Road. Encompassing about twenty-five mature sequoias, the grove also boasts a "driveway," which passes through the base of the Dead Giant. A fallen tree in the grove, known to former students of the Yosemite Institute as "Dead Fred," features a hollow trunk that can be entered at the root-ball and followed to where the bark begins to break open.

The Merced Grove, the smallest and arguably the most remote of the three Yosemite groves, lies off the Big Oak Flat Road farther north of the Tuolumne Grove. Another twenty or so mature giants are harbored here, in a setting that, especially in the less-busy tourist seasons, is seldom crowded.

TREES AS PRODUCT

If you count the Ahwahneechee and their bark homes, lumber has been processed in Yosemite for thousands of years. John Muir, for all that he worshipped the trees, was one of the first white men to make a living off the bounty of Yosemite's woodlands, employed by pioneer James Hutchings to build and work a sawmill on the Valley floor. In Muir's defense, much of the wood he milled was from pines that had blown down in a "violent windstorm"—likely what is now called a Mono Wind. Mono Winds occasionally whip over the Sierra crest during the winter months, and as they are funneled between the ridges, can reach speeds of up to one hundred miles per hour; the winds have caused destruction and a couple of deaths within the Yosemite Valley over the years. Clark estimated that "more than a million board feet of lumber had been leveled by severe storms" in the winter of 1867–1868, according to historian Hank Johnston. The lumber Muir milled was used to build structures on the homesteads of the first Valley residents.

Imagine their delight when timbermen saw the giant sequoia. The board feet that could be milled by some of the biggest sequoias in the Sierra—thankfully still standing—range from 376,000 to more than 600,000, according to a botanical study published by the University of California Press in 1940. By comparison, the biggest coast redwoods have produced, on average, a paltry 155,600 board feet.

But the ancient trees survived the appetite for lumber that decimated redwood forests along the coast in California's frontier days. For all their impressive size, the giant sequoia proved too fragile for commercial interests. The assessment of the UC Berkeley study says it best: "Because of the brittleness of the wood and the wastefulness of lumbering it, the Sierra Redwood is of sentimental rather than commercial importance. So far as actual use is concerned, nearly every timber tree in the United States is superior to it."

Lumberjacks discovered the weakness early on, when some of the giants essentially shattered as they hit the ground. Taking them down to make shake shingles, split rails, and toothpicks wasn't as lucrative as harvesting straight, strong, and useful lumber from a good old sugar pine, or a Douglas fir. While groves of coast redwoods were mowed down in the late nineteenth century—that lumber is prized for its durability—the sequoia groves in the Sierra, once word got around, were mostly spared. That's not to say impressive groves weren't cut. The Fresno Grove, now known as the Nelder Grove, at one time held more than six hundred giant sequoias, according to Clark. The grove was harvested in part, and the wood sent by flume to the flatlands for processing. Despite the losses, the National Park Service counts seventy-five surviving natural groves of giant sequoia in the Sierra Nevada in modern times.

But both the giant sequoia and the coast redwood, even where protected within national and state parks, still face threats. The coast redwood is dependent upon the fog that regularly inundates northern California's oceanfront from the central coast to the Oregon border; the tree cannot survive without it. Scientists surmise that the coast redwood's great height is an adaptation allowing it to harvest maximum moisture from the marine layer from top to bottom. The fear is that, as a result of global climate change, this feast of moisture may be on the wane. The fog banks haven't been as thick or as dense in recent years.

The giant sequoia of the Sierra is also moisture-loving. It's found only on the west side of the range, where Pacific storms dump the most snow and rain; the eastern escarpment is in what's known as the rain shadow, and the terrain there is drier, supporting a desert scrub. With no fog blanket to draw from, the giant sequoia instead uses its sprawling, shallow root system—about six feet under, but extending out more than one hundred feet—and an internal "pump" to draw moisture from the soil to the crown. According to botanists, the sun-powered pumping system moves a ton of water daily from root to canopy. If climate change were to result in prolonged or permanent drought on the western slopes, the trees would be hard-pressed to survive.

Equally significant to the long-term health of giant sequoia groves is fire. Suppressed for more than a century in national forests and national parks, wildfire is essential to the germination of new giant sequoias. The ground fires that burned at regular intervals throughout the Sierra before the era of suppression, which dominated forest management for much of the twentieth century, did three critical things for the giants. It opened the sequoias' cones, allowing the seeds to fall free and germinate. Each of the thousands of egg-shaped cones produced in the crown of a mature giant sequoia contains about two hundred tiny seeds, giving the tree a whopping regenerative potential. Fire also cleared underbrush, allowing sunlight, critical for the survival of sequoia seedlings and saplings, to reach the forest floor. Lastly, the ash left behind by a ground fire fertilized the soil, providing critical nutrients for the young trees. The mature sequoias were hardly fazed by these blazes; their bark, averaging two feet in thickness and shot with tannin, is fire-resistant. That's not to say fire doesn't leave scars, as demonstrated by the blackened hollows, some large enough for bears to den in, borne by many of the giants.

Not to Be Forgotten

As impressive as the giant sequoia are, the other trees of Yosemite are also worthy of a hug or two. They suffered the depredations of settlers and lumbermen to a far greater extent than did the big trees. From the turn of the twentieth century into the 1940s, timber cutting took place on inholdings within the park, as well as on its boundaries. The industry was facilitated by the completion of the Yosemite Valley Railroad in 1907, and lumber companies, such as the Yosemite Sugar Pine Lumber Company (the sugar pine was a favorite, as it also attains impressive heights and girth), built spur lines into the woods to transport timber from forest to mill and construction site.

The value of Yosemites trees shouldn't, however, be measured simply in dollars per board foot. The sugar pine, along with the ponderosa pine, Jeffrey pine, and Douglas fir—all sourced as lumber—form the canopy of a montane zone ecosystem that supports bear, deer, and a number of other creatures. The trees also make up the impressive woodlands that shade trail system on the Yosemite Valley floor.

The incense cedar, a spectacular specimen easily distinguished from other montane zone evergreens by its furrowed bark and the more vibrant green of its needles, was a favorite of John Muir's. "It would be delightful to be storm-bound beneath one of these noble, hospitable, inviting old trees," he wrote in *The Yosemite*, "its broad sheltering arms bent down like a tent, incense rising from the fire made by its dry fallen branches, and a hearty wind chanting overhead." The durable bark was also the construction material of choice for the homes, or *o'chums*, built by Yosemite's Indians before contact. Oaks are also prized montane residents; the California black oak was cultivated by the Indians for acorns, and Muir called the mountain live oak "a sturdy mountaineer of a tree."

A little higher in elevation, in the upper montane zone, yellow pines give way to lodgepole pines and mountain hemlock—still harvestable, but less desirable than their lower-elevation neighbors. Above that, trees are generally not considered a marketable product. In the subalpine zone, the whitebark pine maintains its grip in the cracks of the granite, its stunted trunks and twisted boughs bent under incessant wind. As krummholz, the white pine hunkers carpetlike over the rock at the tree line. White pines don't have commercial value, but are durable in ways no other tree can touch, surviving on windswept dome tops blanketed half the year in snow, providing habitat for the equally hardy creatures that abide, even seasonally, in the subalpine and alpine zones.

The Tree Keeper

There have been many noble Knights of the High Sierras, but Galen Clark was one of the noblest of all.
—Ben C. Truman, in the introduction to Galen Clark's *The Yosemite Valley*

Galen Clark was a sick man when he settled in the mountains along the Indian trail to the Yosemite Valley. He had come from the East Coast, like so many others, hoping to make his fortune in the Sierran goldfields. He'd have no luck as an argonaut, but then again, he'd had no luck before that, either.

According to historian Shirley Sargent's thorough biography, Clark was born in 1814 in Quebec, Canada, part of a large American family that would relocate back to New Hampshire in 1819. The young Clark would, variously, find work as a chair maker, a housepainter, a farmer (an enterprise that "proved disastrous"), and a furniture maker, but struggled in those years with debt and illness. He and his first wife, Rebecca, had five children together before her death in 1848. After that, Clark settled his children with family and set off for California. He hoped, like so many others, for good luck and good fortune in the Golden State.

After arrival in San Francisco in 1853, he set off for the Sierra, tried his hand at prospecting, and found employment in the mines around Mariposa and Sonora. He first traveled to Yosemite as part of a tour group in 1855; shortly thereafter, he filed a claim on a 160-acre homestead off the Indian trail in what would become Wawona. The turning point in his life was a good thing hidden in a bad thing. Clark was working for the Mariposa Ditch Company when consumption (tuberculosis) caused a lung hemorrhage, and he was forced to quit. Famously quoted as saying "I went to the mountains to take my chances of dying or growing better, which I thought were about even," at the age of forty-two, he packed up and retired to the homestead. That's where he'd decided to wait for death.

He ended up waiting a long time: Clark would live to be nearly ninety-six years old. Clean mountain air, good hard work, and long walks in the woods proved his salvation. But just in case, Clark would dig his own grave in the Yosemite Valley in 1886 and plant sequoia seedlings around it, and then dig a well so that he could water those seedlings in the years he had left.

Clark built a humble cabin at the edge of the meadow on his claim in 1857. His good character and generosity resulted in a slow evolution into his becoming the Yosemite Grant's unofficial greeter. The trail through what would become Wawona—long used by the local Indians and traveled by the Mariposa Battalion in the campaign to oust them—had become a primary route into the Yosemite Valley and Mariposa Grove, which were attracting increasing numbers of sightseers and homesteaders. The accommodations Clark offered travelers were primitive, and the food wasn't fancy, but the road was long, and if respite was needed the mountain man was happy to provide.

Clark was also, like many on the frontier in those days, a keen observer and diligent recorder. Though he didn't achieve the fame of a John Muir or a Clarence King, Clark's written records of his explorations among the

Galen Clark and the Grizzly Giant. PHOTO: CARLETON WATKINS. DIGITAL IMAGE COURTESY OF THE GETTY'S OPEN CONTENT PROGRAM.

giant sequoias, published in articles and later in a book titled *The Big Trees of California*, described, as accurately as he was able, the natural attributes of the wilderness he knew better than anyone else at the time.

Clark's meadowland outpost evolved into Clark's Station, and Clark became the primary guide to the Mariposa Grove, leading tourists on the winding tree-lined paths before directing them down to the Valley to see those sights. Among those he guided was poet Ralph Waldo Emerson, who, along with John Muir, would tour the grove in 1871 and help name some of the trees there.

Clark and Muir, having similar interests and motivations, became friends over the years. Clark was, like Muir, a Sierra Club member. The two also wandered in the backcountry together on several occasions, where Clark's skill set and fearlessness matched Muir's. "Galen Clark was the best mountaineer I ever met, and one of the kindest and most amiable of all my mountain friends," Muir wrote.

In *The Yosemite*, Muir describes an adventure the two undertook in the Grand Canyon of the Tuolumne above Hetch Hetchy. They were accompanied by a less-seasoned companion, who balked at following the two old-timers farther upcanyon after making a treacherous river crossing. Clark made that crossing, Muir wrote, by "wading and jumping from one submerged boulder to another through the torrent, bracing and steadying himself with a long pole." One can only imagine the poor young tagalong, humbled and unwilling to proceed, hunkering down as the two wild men continued without him, wondering if Clark and Muir would return to see him safely back to the Valley. Of course, they did.

Clark and Muir shared a love of wilderness, but their expressions of that love differed radically. To understand, you need look no further than their descriptions of the giant sequoia. Muir called Yosemite's sequoias "the king of conifers, the noblest of all the noble race. These colossal trees are as wonderful in fineness of beauty and proportion as in stature—an assemblage of conifers surpassing all that have ever yet been discovered in the forests of the world." In *The Yosemite*, he offers page upon page of poetic and scholarly description. Clark's *Big Trees* is much sparser, chapters sometimes only a few paragraphs long, and is more practical than poetic, cautioning readers, for instance, against being disappointed at the size of the trees. "[One] cause of this occasional sense of disappointment is [the] fact that most of the measurements published are taken at the base of the tree near the ground, which is larger than the body of the tree a few feet above. Persons taking measurements for publication should state whether taken near the ground or how many feet up," Clark wrote.

Clark worked hard to maintain his hotel and guide services as viable businesses, and later joined in a toll-road concern with a partner, Edwin Moore. But his bad luck as a businessman persisted, and he would eventually sell his failing holdings at Wawona. No matter. His life's work had been cut out for him with the passage of the Yosemite Grant Act in 1864.

The act, which placed both the Yosemite Valley and the Mariposa Grove of Big Trees under the oversight of the state of California as protected public reserves, also established a board of commissioners to oversee the grant lands. A guardian was assigned from that board to administer the commissioners' vision for the park on the ground. Clark was appointed both commissioner and guardian, effectively becoming America's first park ranger. He'd serve as guardian from 1864 to 1880, and again from 1890 (reclaiming the spot at the age of seventy-five) to 1897, when he retired because he believed a younger man would be better able to meet the demands of the job.

Clark and fellow commissioner Frederick Law Olmsted, recognized as "the father of landscape architecture in America" and a premier park planner, arguably had the best understanding of the potential that Yosemite and the Mariposa Grove held as a national trust. Olmsted had first visited Yosemite while working on the Mariposa Estate, which state geologist Josiah Whitney described as a "famous quartz-mining estate that [had] many ups and downs." Olmsted had already designed New York's Central Park and other acclaimed public spaces. In his "Preliminary Report on Yosemite and the Mariposa Grove," published in 1865, Olmsted argued that preservation of Yosemite's natural values was integral to the health and well-being of all comers, and that the park should be accessible to everyone, regardless of social or financial status. To accomplish this, Olmsted, on behalf of the commission, argued that suitable and safe public access must be provided. Road building would prove a major thrust in the development of the park in the grant years, as would the provision of adequate lodging for guests. The elimination of private inholdings within the reserve was also key to making sure the new public park was open to all. A policy of ten-year leases was established, and the commission set about acquiring existing land holdings within the grant.

Clark proved masterful in mediating the directives of the commission with Valley residents and landowners—for the most part. He was a mountaineer, but he was also a diplomat. Amid the vitriol and wrangling that accompanied administration of the Yosemite Grant in those years, with lawsuits flying, and road wars, and hotels changing hands like cards in a game of Crazy Eights, hardly a disparaging word appears in the literature about Galen Clark. He would be ordered, over the years, to evict Valley residents and take down buildings that had been erected without the commission's permission. The guardian was the enforcer, but somehow he meted out unpopular decisions without inspiring personal rancor—at least rancor that spilled into the written record. Doubtless his manner, that of a "gentle man," was integral to his success. Muir would write that he never heard Clark "utter a hasty, angry, fault-finding word."

Clark's steady administrative hand ensured that the vision of public access set forth by Olmsted would come to pass, as tourists were, for the most part, safely provided for. That meant the people who ran Yosemite's hotels, saloons, and toll roads had the infrastructure they needed to succeed. The leaseholders of the Valley's hotels and camps were mostly families with children, so among Clark's recommendations to the Yosemite commission was that a school be established. That institution started as a gathering around an oak tree, according to one historian, but by 1907 the dozen or so school-age children in the Valley, including some Indian children, were studying in a proper building.

Though he was considered "popular and effective" as guardian, Clark was ousted, along with the rest of the Yosemite commission, in 1880, unseated by bickering between politicians in the state legislature and commission members, primarily over funding improvements in the Yosemite Grant. But after the tenures of three "disastrous" interim guardians he was reinstated, and continued in the position for another seven years. His office, for the second term, was located in the old Cosmopolitan building, and became a gathering place for Valley denizens. Yosemite National Park, which surrounded the grant lands, had been established by that time, and Clark worked within that framework, paving, in his quiet way, a path toward the next big step in Yosemite's evolution. In 1906 the grant lands were ceded back to the United States, and Yosemite was whole.

Clark remained a resident of the Valley even after the Yosemite Grant was rolled into the national park. As an old man he would become a snowbird, dividing his time between a home by the sea near Santa Barbara and Yosemite. In the park he served as a tour guide and managed summer camps, becoming known as "Mr. Yosemite," and called "a ranger who worked without a paycheck." His books were written after his retirement as well. First came *Indians of Yosemite Valley and Vicinity* (1904); *The Big Trees of California* was published in 1907. *The Yosemite Valley*, published in 1910, was sent to the publisher just weeks before Clark was "summoned to his last account."

Yosemite guardian Galen Clark reclines next to the Merced.

The books, like many others written by his contemporaries, are essentially guides, though Clark's descriptions are Hemingway-esque in their brevity. Take his "Hints for Yosemite Visitors:" Without preamble, he sets forth a list of tips, suggesting that "[s]moked glasses will sometimes save the wearer a headache," that "an umbrella is apt to be a useless encumbrance" in all but four months of the year, and that while walking, "keep your mouth shut, and breathe through your nose. Talk all you wish while stopping for a short rest." He also suggests that visitors bring more money than they might expect, since they might want to stay longer in the Valley, and that, of course, they bring a camera.

Though Galen Clark died at his daughter's home in Oakland, he is, as he planned, buried in the Yosemite Cemetery, in the grave he dug himself a half-century before, beneath a granite stone upon which his name is carved, and surrounded by his precious sequoias. Mount Clark, the Clark Range, Clark Point on the John Muir Trail, and the Galen Clark Tree in the Mariposa Grove are all named in his honor. The man who came to the mountains to meet his end did so only after making the map.

Wawona

The original meaning of the Indian word *Wawona* is in some dispute. In the literature it is translated variously as "big tree" or "big pine tree"; the hoot of an owl, which was thought to be a protector of the big trees ("*who-who'nau*"); the place of the "wah wah men," a tribelet of the Miwok; and "evening primrose." Like Yosemite, also known as Ahwahnee, Wawona had an entirely separate Indian identity, as *Pallachun*, "a good place to stop." Regardless its etymology, by 1882, with Galen Clark Yosemite's guardian, and the Washburn family having established its lodging and sightseeing concession at the site, Clark's Station was no more. The name Wawona, whatever it meant, had stuck.

Human occupation of the area predates contact, though the first historical accounts of Wawona as a village don't appear until the Mariposa Battalion came through in 1851. The Nutchu Indians camped in the meadows near the Mariposa Grove for many years, but they, like the Yosemite Indians, were forced to abandon the site as settlers moved in. Clark was among the first homesteaders, and walked softly and alone on the land for a short time. Then the Mann brothers came through, improving the Indian trail that connected the Nutchu to the Yosemite Valley and to the flatlands as a toll road.

After Clark became guardian, he let go his foundering business enterprises at Wawona. He had encumbered himself with significant debt to take a stab at building a toll road from the woodland settlement to the Valley, and when he was unable to make the payments on that debt, he sold the concern, his acreage, and his station house to the Washburn brothers.

Henry, John, and Edward Washburn, fortune-seekers who had come west from Vermont, were "stalwart, bearded men with pioneering, adventurous spirits," according to historian Sargent. The brothers proved diligent and creative in their development of Wawona. Access to the Yosemite Valley from the south side was critical to the success of their enterprise, so Henry Washburn set to work improving the toll road he had acquired from Clark and partner Edwin Moore. Wagon roads would reach the Valley floor from the north side in 1874, and Washburn wasn't far behind.

For the most part, the Wawona wagon road followed the long-established trail, and Washburn didn't wait until the improvements were complete before he sent people down the mountain. When construction on a stretch of roadway across an unstable slope impeded travel, stagecoach passengers "disembarked to walk past the construction area," writes historian Hank Johnston. "At the same time, workmen dismantled the stage and carried the pieces by hand to the opposite side of the incomplete section, where it was speedily reassembled and sent on its way. Not only did passengers not seem to mind the inconvenience, [but] it was reported that many travelers actually chose the southern route because of the novel portage." The road reached the Valley floor in 1875, and today's Wawona Road/CA 41 essentially follows the same route.

The Washburns' most significant development was the Wawona Hotel, a National Historic Landmark still in operation today. The hotel property and surrounding village were developed over several decades. First came the Long White, or Clark's Cottage, which opened for business in 1876. The main hotel, with its two-story, covered verandah and the cones of giant sequoias incorporated into the light fixtures, was completed

A stage negotiates the steep and dusty Wawona Road. COURTESY OF THE YOSEMITE NATIONAL PARK ARCHIVES, MUSEUM, AND LIBRARY

in 1879. Other buildings followed, including the Little White, used as a manager's cottage; the Long Brown; the Little Brown; and the studio of artist Thomas Hill, whose daughter would marry John Washburn. The Annex came last, completed in 1918. Three fountains added ambience to the already lovely setting; two of the fountains have been restored, one within the bounds of the hotel's circular drive, and the second at the Hill studio. The enterprise, which operated only in the summer months and offered rooms, meals, and tours, earned praise from many Yosemite travelers and quickly, quietly, became an institution.

When Yosemite National Park was established in 1890, Camp A. E. Wood at Wawona became headquarters for cavalry and infantry units assigned to patrol and caretake the new parklands. In addition to the camp, the army built an arboretum and a fish hatchery at the site. When the Yosemite Grant, including the Mariposa Grove of Big Trees, was ceded back under federal oversight, army headquarters relocated to Fort Yosemite on the Valley floor. The arboretum was abandoned, and the camp was converted to civilian use.

The Wawona Hotel, pictured here in 1898, still welcomes visitors to the park.
PHOTO: W. H. JACKSON. COURTESY OF THE YOSEMITE NATIONAL PARK ARCHIVES, MUSEUM, AND
LIBRARY.

The Washburn property, however, remained outside the park boundaries until 1932, when Clarence Washburn, son of brother John, sold the family business and property to the park. The Yosemite Park and Curry Company, concessionaire at the time, took over the operation. With that, Wawona, once Clark's Station, portal to the Mariposa Grove of Big Trees, and long the southern gateway to Yosemite National Park, was folded into the public domain.

John Muir:
The Wanderer Who Was Never Lost

Like the landscape that inspired him, John Muir is legendary, enduring, and radiant. At a glance the story seems simple—a man and his mountains—but the man was as complex as the Range of Light he championed. The Sierra Nevada is peaks and valleys, swift rivers and quiet alpine tarns, meadows and forests, sharp granite and soft grasses. Muir was a hobo wandering in the woods and a sophisticate, a gentleman farmer and a naturalist, a husband and father, an activist and an author. In the contrasts of his life, as in the contrasts of the mountains, there was a brilliant synergy.

Muir's wandering shoes carried him thousands of miles across America's loveliest wildernesses, from the redwood forests of northern California to the sun-hued deserts of the Southwest; to Alaska; to the Grand Canyon; and before all that, on a thousand-mile walk from Wisconsin to Florida. But Yosemite was his muse, and colored his life in extraordinary ways.

His Boyhood and Youth

When I was a boy in Scotland I was fond of everything that was wild, and all my life I've been growing fonder and fonder of wild places and wild creatures.
—from The Story of My Boyhood and Youth

From his earliest days, John Muir sought the wild life. As a child and young man, that wasn't easy to do, with his days dedicated to labor and, whenever possible, study. But his memoir of those early days, *The Story of My Boyhood and Youth*, is as full of stories of wonder and discovery by the sea and in the woods as it is of hard work and family life.

Born in Dunbar, Scotland, on April 21, 1838, he was the third child and the eldest son of Daniel Muir and his wife, Anne. His younger brother David, in those early years, was his companion in adventure. Muir describes exploring the rugged shoreline of the frigid North Sea with his brother and friends, "bathing" in swirling pools among the rocks, racing for miles through the countryside, and climbing everything in sight, including the exterior of his home. He was such a good climber as a boy, he wrote, that when he "first heard of hell from a servant girl who loved to tell of its horrors, I always insisted that I could climb out of it."

But it wasn't all fun and games. His upbringing was strict and regimented, dominated by a righteous and God-fearing father. He started school at three, and when he wasn't studying from lesson books, he was memorizing the Bible. Discipline was maintained with "thrashings," doled out for any infraction. Muir is matter-of-fact about the beatings and the domineering; they were simply part of his Scotch upbringing, to be endured and, whenever possible, avoided.

Daniel Muir emigrated to America in 1849, when John Muir was ten years old. He took Sarah, one of his older daughters, John, and David with him, and would bring his wife and the rest of the children (the youngest, Joanna, would be born in America) over once the family homestead had been established and a suitable house built. The California gold rush was under way, but the senior Muir wasn't headed that far west. He settled the family on a parcel of woodland on Fountain Lake in western Wisconsin, where he and his children would clear farmland and raise potatoes, wheat, and corn.

John Muir and his siblings spent their days in hard labor on the Fountain Lake farm. "We were all made slaves through the service of over-industry," he wrote of the hardships of the enterprise. And when that farmland was developed and producing, the elder Muir purchased a new half-section, dubbed Hickory Hill Farm, a move that, in Muir's words, "[doubled] all the stunting, heart-breaking chipping, grubbing, stump-digging, rail-splitting, fence-building, barn-building, house-building, and so forth."

Nevertheless, young John somehow found time during those years to watch the birds, squirrels, deer, gophers, and coons (even if his task was to hunt them), to learn to swim (and nearly drown), and to observe, in great detail, the lay of the land and how the trees, flowers, and grasses grew upon it. Later, he would sacrifice sleep to read poetry, teach himself higher math, and invent things, building clocks, barometers, thermometers, and other gadgetry all from wood.

That inventiveness would enable Muir, as a young man, to escape the family farm. He brought his whittled wooden clocks to the state fair in 1860 and won acclaim, a little money, and a job offer. That job didn't last long, however, as Muir was set on higher education. Despite his lack of formal schooling, he was able to enter the University of Wisconsin, Madison, where he studied botany and geology. He paid his way with money he earned working on the farm through the summer, and spent a winter teaching school as well.

In his time at the University of Wisconsin, Muir established lifelong friendships with Professor Ezra Carr and his wife, Jeanne, who would become a faithful correspondent. These two mentored the young inventor and naturalist, encouraging him first in his mechanical endeavors, and later in his preservation efforts. They also introduced him to his wife, Louisa.

Muir had become a student just as the country plunged into the Civil War; he would leave the university—without a degree, but with his love of scientific observation firmly established—as that war wound down. He'd dreamed of being an inventor or a physician, but he had the heart of an explorer. Though he recognized the university had more to offer, he "wandered away on a glorious botanical and geological excursion," that would last the rest of his life. He left the "Wisconsin University for the University of the Wilderness."

Before he began wandering in earnest, however, Muir detoured into machine work, finding employment in shops in Canada, and, later, in Indianapolis. In the latter position, while making a repair to a circular saw, he suffered a severe eye injury. For a time he was completely blind; his right eye, he feared, was "gone, closed forever to all God's beauty," and the other eye darkened "by sympathy." The injury healed, his vision returned, and with it came renewed clarity. The young Muir took stock and then took off, setting out on "a thousand-mile walk to the Gulf of Mexico" that would take him through half a dozen states to Florida, and then, if all went as planned, on to Cuba and South America.

The Incomparable Yosemite

Oh, these vast, calm, measureless mountain days, days in whose light everything seems equally divine, opening a thousand windows to show us God. Nevermore, however weary, should one faint by the way who gains the blessings of one mountain day; whatever his fate, long life, short life, stormy or calm, he is rich forever.
—from My First Summer in the Sierra

John Muir's first journey did not end as planned. He made it to Florida, then contracted a fever that precluded his continuing south.

Yosemite would be his cure.

In April 1868 he set out from Oakland with an English companion named Chilwell for the acclaimed Yosemite Valley. Broke, without prospects, and seeking an unorthodox route, he simply started walking. He was looking for a wild place and he found it: first, California's Great Valley, a "flower garden" unrivaled in his experience, then the foothills surrounding the Merced River as it flowed from Yosemite. On his first view of the Valley, as yet unaware of "Yosemite's magnitudes," he would call the Bridalveil a "dainty little fall" that looked, from his vantage point, no more than sixty or seventy feet high. He and his fellow traveler would spend "eight or ten days" exploring the Valley, and camp in the Mariposa Grove. It was, for Muir, an abbreviated ramble, but transformative.

In his first summer in the Sierra, in 1869, Muir would help lead a flock of sheep to summer grazing in Tuolumne Meadows. He had agreed to help a Mr. Delaney guide the sheep to high country forage with the promise that he'd be able to study the flora and geology along the route. The path took him over the range via the divide between the Tuolumne and Merced Rivers. He did his part as a sheepherder, helping chase down strays and fend off the bears that raided the camps to feast on mutton. But he was truly studying, sketching the plants and trees, noting the glacial attributes of the rocks, testing and honing his mountaineering skills. He would skitter down from a camp near Tenaya Lake into the Valley to meet one of his professors from the university, then climb back to the heights and continue on to Tuolumne Meadows. He'd also travel down the east side of the range, following Bloody Canyon to Mono Lake.

For a few short years, from 1869 to 1873, Muir made Yosemite his home, finding work at James Hutchings's sawmill, as the caretaker of Black's Hotel below Sentinel Rock, guiding tourists on tramps into the canyons and up to the rim. He also continued to study the nature of the place, and began to publish articles, the first being a description of Yosemite's glaciers in the *New York Tribune*. He would compose a beautiful tribute to his time in the park many years later in *The Yosemite*. The book is the ultimate guide to Yosemite in a wilder time, a place where Muir—and anyone else, for that matter—could lose themselves in the forest, on the cliffs, among the peaks on the divide.

Even as a young man, Muir was likely the most well-educated walker in the woods in those pioneering days. He was able to identify many of the flowering plants, shrubs, and evergreens that he encountered, and to decipher how the rock he strode across was formed; if he didn't know, he would study it until he figured it out, and then he would write about it.

But for all his research, his grand body of work, and his long life, the young Muir did things that most modern mortals wouldn't dare, even those who might scale the sheer walls of El Capitan (with rope, harness, and a good belay, of course). The stories that he sprinkles among his scholarly observations are enough to make the most stalwart mother's hair stand on end, and his exploits would have scrambled the national park's search-and-rescue teams if they had existed at the time.

In one instance, Muir recounts climbing barefoot and barehanded along rushing Yosemite Creek to find the bitter edge, where he hoped to be able to survey the Yosemite Valley from a perch at the brink of Yosemite Falls. He reached a slope even he deemed too dangerous to attempt, and then dropped down it anyway, onto a ledge just wide enough to plant his heels. From here he "obtained a perfectly free view down into the heart of the snowy, chanting throng of comet-like streamers . . . the tremendous grandeur of the fall in form and sound and motion, acting at close range, smothered the sense of fear."

On another occasion he ventured behind the fall at night, seeking to admire the view of a full moon from behind the veil. Taking advantage of the wind, which moved the fall back like a curtain, he found himself "in fairyland between the dark wall and the wild throng of illumined waters." His enchantment was short-lived, however; the wind changed, the fall crashed back into place, and Muir was subjected to an icy pummeling that forced him to curl up "like a young fern frond with my face pressed against my breast." He eventually was able to escape, and, after a couple hours' sleep, pronounced himself "better, not worse, for my midnight bath."

And, in the wake of the "earthquake storm" that broke along the eastern Sierra in 1872, fearless (or ignorant) of aftershocks, Muir witnessed a wall collapse on Eagle Rock, "a terribly sublime spectacle." He ran to the newly created talus field, where the boulders "were slowly settling into their places, chafing, grating against one another, groaning," his curiosity about the geologic forces that created talus overriding common sense.

The quintessential guidebook writer, Muir's stamina as a trekker is epitomized in the hike suggestions he makes near the end of *The Yosemite*. His idea of a nice day hike begins by climbing out of the Valley and ascending Sentinel Dome, traversing to Glacier Point, dropping back toward the Valley floor via Illilouette Creek above Illilouette Fall, curling around to Nevada Fall, taking a little detour to the top of Liberty Cap, and then heading down past Vernal Fall to complete the loop. The hike from Glacier Point down to the Valley floor via what is now the Panorama and John Muir Trails is a relatively common undertaking for modern Valley visitors (albeit, most often without the summit of Liberty Cap), but only the heartiest hikers, or the most inexperienced, take it on.

John Muir's vagabond days ended when he left the Valley in 1874. His wandering would continue, but now with purpose. His writings had appeared in periodicals across the nation, and his reputation as a naturalist and wilderness advocate was blossoming. He would return to Yosemite many times over the course of his life, but never as a poor man, and never as an unknown.

The Gentleman Farmer

The mountains are calling, and I must go.
—from a letter to his sister, Sarah, written in 1873

Through his good friend Jeanne Carr, wife of his University of Wisconsin professor Ezra Carr, John Muir would make the acquaintance of Louisa Strentzel, called Louie, in 1874. By that time he had moved out of Yosemite and into the San Francisco Bay Area, where he focused on writing articles about his continuing travels in the mountains of California and beyond. Louie was the daughter of Dr. John and Mrs. Louisiana Strentzel. Dr. Strentzel was a Polish immigrant who had established a fruit farm in the Alhambra Valley, in what is now the San Francisco/Oakland suburb of Martinez. John and Louie married in 1880; he was just shy of forty-two, and she was thirty-three.

Louie was well-educated and an accomplished pianist, but she was no fan of the wilderness that so inspired her husband. She made a single trip with him to Yosemite, where, according to a biographer, she "mistook trout for catfish, didn't like hiking about, and saw bears behind every tree." In addition, her husband "grumbled" about the amount of luggage she traveled with. But she supported and believed in Muir, enabling him to continue his studies and preservation work by maintaining the ranch when he was absent.

Muir would spend ten years diligently running the Strentzel family farm in the Alhambra Valley. The fruit ranch consisted of 2,600 acres, and was planted with more than a thousand varieties of fruit—orchards of apples, apricots, pears, and plums—which had been bred and planted by his father-in-law, a noted horticulturalist. Muir amassed a fortune in those years, his inventiveness and background on the farms in Wisconsin providing a solid foundation for his success, augmented by discipline and the fertility of California's soil. At his death, the farm was worth an estimated $250,000, the equivalent of $5 million today.

During those years, Muir and his wife had two daughters, Wanda and Helen. The father delighted in the girls, and would name two "mountains" for them, high points on the Alhambra Valley ranch crowned with views that stretch eastward past the twin peaks of Mount Diablo toward the distant summits of his Range of Light.

The house he lived in with Louie and his daughters, and later, his sister, Mary, an artist, is a grand Italianate with a bell tower atop, open to the sea breezes and views in every direction. Built by Dr. Strentzel in 1882, the home is elegant but modest, particularly the parlor in which Muir entertained his fellow wilderness advocates—businessmen, politicians, writers, and artists. Muir remodeled the house after it was damaged in the 1906 earthquake, redoing one of the parlors in earth tones and building a large, brick fireplace suitable for a mountaineer, the room decorated only with paintings depicting his favorite wildernesses for inspiration. Steep

John Muir with wife, Louie, and daughters Helen and Wanda on the Martinez farm, circa 1900. COURTESY OF THE JOHN MUIR NATIONAL HISTORIC SITE, JOMU1732

staircases lead from one floor to the next, and one can imagine, on those days when the aging hiker's knees were particularly creaky, him leaning more heavily on the polished bannister that ran alongside. The Strentzel mansion is now the focal point of the John Muir National Historic Site, which also encompasses an adobe house that dates to the gold rush.

Though Louie doesn't loom large in the mythology of John Muir, her unfailing support enabled him to pursue his passion, and that bespeaks a solid partnership that was private and caring. When Muir began to founder near the end of the 1880s, he would seek renewal by climbing Mount Rainier. While he was away, Louie sent him a letter encouraging his return to travel and writing. "A ranch that needs and takes the sacrifice of a noble life, or work, ought to be flung away beyond all reach," she wrote. "The Alaska book and the Yosemite book, dear John, must be written, and you need to be your own self, well and strong to make them worthy of you." Within a year he was again on a tramp to Alaska, and also embarked on a campaign to protect the Yosemite Valley, the Mariposa Grove, and surrounding landscapes as a national park.

But the Alhambra Valley ranch, and the family he helped build there, remained Muir's anchor into old age. Louie would die in 1905, and her husband would continue his travels upon her passing, but he always came back to the family home.

Friendship, Travel, and the Pen

These mountain fires that glow in one's blood are free to all, but I cannot find the chemistry that may press them unimpaired into booksellers' bricks.
—from a letter to Jeanne Carr, written in 1872

He did it well, but by all accounts, John Muir didn't enjoy writing.

On the other hand, he was a popular and effective storyteller. Given a campfire, an intelligent listener or two (or more), and a subject about which he was passionate, Muir's ability to enchant was legendary.

Muir's career as writer and wilderness advocate began while he was in Yosemite, with the publication of an article in the *New York Tribune* in 1871. In the article he argued that the remarkable architecture of the Yosemite Valley had been carved by glaciers, which contradicted the determination of California's state geologist Josiah Whitney, among others. These esteemed experts believed the Valley was formed by "subsidence" that had occurred when the floor of the Valley collapsed as the Sierra Nevada were lifted up. Muir's article drew fire, and fire drew recognition. In the end, Muir would be proven right. But in the controversy, his career was launched.

Over the years, he would publish 150 articles on all manner of subjects related to natural history and the preservation of parklands and woodlands, from descriptions of water ouzels frolicking in waterfalls and his adventure at the top of a Douglas fir in a windstorm, to advocacy for the establishment of a national park service and in opposition to building a dam in the Hetch Hetchy Valley. His pieces were published in magazines and newspapers across the country, including the *Overland Monthly*, the *San Francisco Bulletin*, *Scribner's*, the *Atlantic*, *Century* magazine, the *New York Tribune*, and, of course, once founded, the *Sierra Club Bulletin*.

The books came later in life, composed at the behest of friends who recognized that a permanent record of Muir's travels and studies would be of lasting importance to Yosemite, the Sierra Club, the fledgling national park system, and wilderness advocacy in general. Despite his difficulty with the process, the volumes would spool out of Muir's pen; it's almost as if the man had so well prepared the stories in his head that they were able to emerge fully formed on the page. *The Mountains of California* was published in 1894, *Our National Parks* in 1901, *Stickeen* in 1909, *My First Summer in the Sierra* in 1911, *The Yosemite* in 1912, and *The Story of My Boyhood and Youth* in 1913. He was editor of *Picturesque California*, a "coffee table" book that included works by other writers along with his own. Titles would be published posthumously as well, including *Travels in Alaska*, *A Thousand-Mile Walk to the Gulf*, and *Steep Trails*.

Even as his books tell the stories of his life and travels, each is also a guide. He teaches as he writes, carefully describing birds, bears, trees, plants, flowers, waterfalls, and rocks as he found them. He documents as much as he rhapsodizes, though it is the rhapsody that touches and inspires.

And then there were the letters and journals, which would be collected by admirers and scholars, including members of the Sierra Club, and published in additional volumes. In these letters Muir's passion for the wildlands and for study, and his affection for his correspondents, comes to the fore. There's no teacher here, no lesson in botany; just kind words and honest observations.

It's not hard to imagine the man, confined to the "scribbling den" in his mansion on the hill, under deadline, twitching in his chair as he bends over his desk. Looking up from that desk out the windows, he would see the green hills of San Francisco's East Bay rolling away—not glaciers, not mountain meadows, not the cliffs of Yosemite, but beckoning just the same, a different flavor of wanderer's paradise. On the walls and over the mantel, above the packed bookshelves, paintings of Yosemite Falls and other iconic landscapes were hung. He surrounded himself within inspiration to offset the burden of the piles of paper he churned out. Typewritten transcriptions of his handwritten musings were made by his wife, daughters, and others, using the Oliver typewriter preserved in his study.

Then off he would go again, to another corner of the world, to explore another unknown landscape. Muir was, until his dying day, a wanderer. He made a number of trips to Alaska, where he would solidify his theory that Yosemite's architecture was executed by glaciers. He would explore the American Southwest, where he would champion preservation of the Grand Canyon and the Petrified Forest, both of which were designated national monuments by President Theodore Roosevelt, and later named national parks by Congress. He would tour a number of European countries. And he made it to South America and the Amazon when he was in his early seventies, where he saw firsthand the geologic and botanical bonanza he'd sought so many years before, and walked a thousand miles to reach.

Muir may have made an "enemy" in Whitney, but his friends were a powerful and formidable force, his biggest advocates in every quest he undertook. Some he met in his Yosemite days, including artist William Keith, who would connect him to the *Overland Monthly*, writer and philosopher Ralph Waldo Emerson, whom Muir greatly admired, and geologist Joseph LeConte of the University of California, Berkeley, a founding

John Muir with friend and colleague John Swett, founder of the California Teachers Association. COURTESY OF THE JOHN MUIR NATIONAL HISTORIC SITE, JOMU 4880 E1-18

member of the Sierra Club and a supporter of Muir's theory of the glacial formation of Yosemite Valley. He also met Asa Gray, the "father of American botany," and traveled with him at the interface of the Sierra Nevada and the Cascade ranges, around Lassen Peak and Mount Shasta. John Swett, a teacher who would establish the California Teachers Association, was another Yosemite acquaintance. Muir would stay with Swett and his wife when in the San Francisco Bay Area, and eventually the two became neighbors in the Alhambra Valley.

In Yosemite Muir came to know and walk with Galen Clark, "the best mountaineer I ever met." The two explored the canyon of the Tuolumne, where Muir would witness Clark's skill in fording the rushing river; they also climbed Mount Lyell together, and set stakes in the McClure glacier to track its movement.

Some friendships would come later, but still have great sway in the course of Muir's life's work. Lawyer William Colby served as the secretary of the Sierra Club during Muir's tenure as president, and was instrumental in helping Muir wage the fight against San Francisco's plan to dam the

Tuolumne River in Hetch Hetchy. The naturalist's unlikely alliance with E. H. Harriman, the Southern Pacific railroad magnate, was cemented when Muir was part of Harriman's 1899 expedition to Alaska. Harriman brought a businessman's practicality to the friendship: He wanted to promote access to the national parks with his railroads. In 1907 Harriman persuaded Muir, then in his late sixties, to begin his autobiography, hiring a stenographer to ease the process, since Muir took more easily to talk than to deskwork. *My Boyhood and Youth* resulted from that collaboration.

Muir also enjoyed a great friendship with fellow conservationist John Burroughs; the two would travel together frequently, and become known as the "two Johnnies." Another close friend was Robert Underwood Johnson, to whom *The Yosemite* is dedicated. Johnson was the publisher of *Century* magazine, in which Muir's work would appear regularly.

His most famous association was with President Theodore Roosevelt. Muir came to Roosevelt's attention after the publication of *Our National Parks* in 1901; a pivotal meeting of the two great minds would take place in 1903 around campfires beneath the Grizzly Giant in the Mariposa Grove, atop Glacier Point in a snowstorm, and in Bridalveil Meadow. In praising the value of wild places to the president, and in arguing for the inclusion of Yosemite Valley and the giant sequoias of Wawona in Yosemite National Park, Muir was essentially preaching to the choir, for Roosevelt had years of exploring and adventuring under his belt, and was already enamored of wild places. The president's legacy as a conservationist includes the establishment of five national parks, twenty-three national monuments, and the setting aside of nearly 150 million

President Theodore Roosevelt and John Muir pose for a photo at Glacier Point in 1903, with the panorama of Yosemite as backdrop. COURTESY OF THE YOSEMITE NATIONAL PARK ARCHIVES, MUSEUM, AND LIBRARY

acres of land as national forests. After meeting with Muir, Roosevelt would sanction the recession of Yosemite Valley and the Mariposa Grove from the state of California to the new national park system in 1906.

THE ADVOCATE

Not blind opposition to progress, but opposition to blind progress.
—JOHN MUIR

He is heralded as the father of the National Park Service, an idea born in his study and brought to fruition in 1916. He would be influential in the establishment of seven national parks and monuments during his lifetime, among them Yosemite, Mount Rainier, the Petrified Forest, the Grand Canyon, and Muir Woods, a tiny pocket of coastal redwoods that, along with a glacier in Alaska and a 211-mile-long stretch of trail along the crest of the high Sierra, bears his name. His books have inspired generations of conservationists. John Muir's legacy thrives in many places and in many ways, but perhaps most vibrantly in the Sierra Club.

Muir and friends founded the club in 1892, and he would serve as president until his death in 1914. The idea behind the club, at the time, was "[t]o explore, enjoy, and render accessible the mountain regions of the Pacific Coast; to publish authentic information concerning them; to enlist the support and co-operation of the people and the Government in preserving the forests and other natural features of the Sierra Nevada Mountains."

Ultimately the Sierra Club would expand its reach across the United States and globally, but the mission remains the same—the preservation of wild places for the pleasure of all people. Central to that mission was the *Sierra Club Bulletin* (now *Sierra* magazine); with the publication, the club still persuades and influences through the power of the pen. The club also sponsored annual outings in the Sierra called "High Trips," to expose and convert "city-weary folks into lovers of, and protectors of, mountains and wilderness."

Walking and writing. It was Muir all over.

For all the ongoing successes, Muir and the Sierra Club did know failure. The fight to save Hetch Hetchy was the naturalist's last political

John Muir in Yosemite in 1907. PHOTO: F. FULTZ. COURTESY OF THE
YOSEMITE NATIONAL PARK ARCHIVES, MUSEUM, AND LIBRARY.

campaign, and would consume his final years. His death would follow
quickly on the passage of the Raker Act in 1913, which gave San Francisco the go-ahead to flood the "Tuolumne Yosemite." Though the cause
was, technically, pneumonia, many students of Muir contend that he died
of a broken heart.

The Sierra Club, however, has endured, and the conviction that
national parks should be "inviolate" remains central to its mission. In the

1920s, the club defeated proposals to build dams in Yellowstone National Park and on the Kings River near Kings Canyon National Park; it would also be part of successful opposition to build dams in Glacier National Park, Dinosaur National Monument, and the Grand Canyon.

Muir also would not live to see the wilderness he so loved protected as fully as he would have wanted. In *The Yosemite*, he expresses concern about overuse of the most sublime of the park's great landmarks. Of Half Dome he writes, "For my part I should prefer leaving it in pure wildness, though, after all, no great damage could be done by tramping over it. The surface would be strewn with tin cans and bottles, but the winter gales would blow the rubbish away. Avalanches might strip off any sort of stairway or ladders that might be built. Blue jays and Clark crows have trodden the Dome for many a day, and so have beetles and chipmunks, and Tissiack would hardly be more 'conquered' or spoiled should man be added to her list of visitors."

He did not—perhaps could not—have imagined the thickets of men and women who would ascend to the summit of the dome as the twentieth century gave way to the twenty-first. So many would come, in fact, that the park has come to limit the number to keep the climb safe and to preserve its "wilderness character." The numbers are still staggering: When the cables are up, three hundred people per day can enter a lottery to obtain a permit to climb.

For all his many talents, Muir could not have foreseen the pressures that would come to bear on America's wildlands. Even as they were preserved they were threatened, by overuse, pollution, political will. But he was prescient in the formation of the Sierra Club, which could, by harnessing the voices of its many members, carry forward his vision of preservation and conservation.

IN THE END

John Muir spent his final days working on a book about his travels in Alaska and struggling with recurrent illness. In a letter to Helen, his youngest daughter, he would write: "I find I take a little cold every time I venture down to the city." He planned to visit Helen at her home in southern California in the winter of 1914, but delayed the trip to avoid catching a bug. It didn't work. He contracted double pneumonia while in the southland, and passed away in a Los Angeles hospital on Christmas Eve.

His obituary in the *New York Times* laid out the accolades and appointments Muir accumulated in his last decades, which were extraordinary considering the man never finished his formal education: "Institutions of learning began to shower honors on the nature lover; Harvard conferred the honorary degree of Master of Arts on him in 1896, the University of Wisconsin followed in 1897 with the LL.D. degree, and the same degree was conferred by the University of California a little more than a year ago. Yale in 1911 conferred the degree of Doctor of Literature upon him. He became a member of the Washington Academy of Science, President of the Sierra Club, a member of the American Alpine Club, of the National Institute of Arts and Letters, of the American Academy of Arts and Letters, and a Fellow of the American Association for the Advancement of Science."

In the end, John Muir's legacy is that of the penultimate wilderness guide. What should one look for in the backyard, in the town, in the wilderness, in the world? How should one explore the backyard, the town, the wilderness, the world? How should one behave toward the backyard, the town, the wilderness, the world? He shows one way to do all these things—a fine, honorable way, illuminated in word and action, true for all time.

Climb the mountains and get their good tidings. Nature's peace will flow into you as sunshine flows into trees. The winds will blow their own freshness into you, and the storms their energy, while cares will drop off like autumn leaves.

—JOHN MUIR

Hetch Hetchy

Dam Hetch Hetchy! As well dam for water-tanks the people's cathedrals and churches, for no holier temple has ever been consecrated by the heart of man.

—JOHN MUIR

THE TUOLUMNE RIVER BEGINS LIKE ALL GREAT RIVERS, NARROW AND ostensibly fragile, deep in an alpine watershed, crossed in a single step.

And the Tuolumne ends where all rivers end—in the sea.

But the Tuolumne does not follow a typical river's course to the Pacific. It winds down from Yosemite's stunning high country into the Hetch Hetchy Valley, where a wall built of concrete and politics stops it short, backs it up, then portions it into pipelines and tunnels that funnel it into the taps of San Franciscans 160 miles downstream.

The O'Shaughnessy Dam in Hetch Hetchy breached what many, most notably John Muir and the Sierra Club, understood to be the "inviolate" status of the nation's fledgling national parks. The city of San Francisco saw things differently. Blame for the conflagration that destroyed much of the city following the 1906 earthquake fell, in part, on an inadequate water supply. Damming the Tuolumne River at the mouth of the Hetch Hetchy Valley, creating a reservoir specifically for the city, was the answer. Later, the record would show that San Francisco's water supply had been more than adequate to quench the fires; it was the failure of the distribution system that hindered the city's firefighting capabilities.

And so the hard questions remain in debate. Was there a need for a dam at that time, in that place, for that purpose? Hetch Hetchy was, and still is, the epicenter of one of the most durable controversies in California's wicked water wars.

YOSEMITE VALLEY'S TUOLUMNE TWIN

Hetch Hetchy is a wonderfully exact counterpart of Yosemite Valley.
—JOHN MUIR

The story of the Hetch Hetchy Valley in the days before the arrival of Europeans parallels that of the Yosemite Valley. Located less than twenty miles north as the crow flies, Hetch Hetchy too was sculpted by glaciers, which took eons to carve monstrous domes and a narrow, flat floor where a river could meander. Where side streams encountered cliffs they crashed down as waterfalls, with Wapama and Tueeulala among the most spectacular in today's Yosemite National Park.

Great trees grew alongside the Tuolumne as it exited its Grand Canyon, finding purchase where the flow mellowed and the fertile river bottom spread—sugar pine, incense cedar, Douglas fir, and the California black oak, which provided the Tuolumne Band of the Me-Wuk with the acorns that were fundamental to their meals. Meadowlands bloomed with grasses and wildflowers in season, including the edible *hetchetci*, from which some claim the valley takes its name.

Even its "discovery" has parallels to that of the Yosemite Valley. The first Europeans to see Hetch Hetchy were, according to one historian, Joseph and Nathan Screech, who wandered into the valley in the late 1840s while hunting bear.

But though it had the domes, and the river, and the waterfalls, Hetch Hetchy did not capture the hearts and minds of visitors in the same way that the Yosemite Valley did. It was not included in the Yosemite Grant of 1864, and it did not see the kind of development or tourist traffic that the Yosemite Valley would see as the nineteenth century proceeded. Hetch Hetchy would, however, be protected within the boundaries of Yosemite National Park as established in 1890—and, ironically, has been part of the park longer than the Yosemite Valley and Mariposa Grove of Big Trees, which weren't added until the act of recession in 1906.

Hetch Hetchy's relative lack of glamour didn't stop John Muir from falling in love with it. He would explore the Valley, along with the Tuolumne's Grand Canyon, which links the Hetch Hetchy to

Tuolumne Meadows, in the years he spent living in the high Sierra at the end of the 1860s and the start of the 1870s. He published articles praising the Valley's beauty and documenting its flora and fauna, using his trademark reverent prose. Describing the Tuolumne as it flowed into Hetch Hetchy, Muir wrote: "[It] is one wild, exulting, on-rushing mass of snow purple bloom, spreading over glacial waves of granite without any definite channel, gliding in magnificent silver plumes, dashing and foaming through huge boulder-dams, leaping high into the air in wheel-like whirls, displaying glorious enthusiasm, tossing from side to side, doubling, glinting, singing in exuberance of mountain energy."

Muir also instigated the idea of the twinship of the valleys, likening Hetch Hetchy's Kolana Rock to Yosemite's Cathedral Rocks, Hetch Hetchy Dome to El Capitan, and Hetch Hetchy's Tueeulala Fall to Yosemite's Bridalveil. Muir was not the only one who found the northern valley enchanting. Josiah Whitney, then California's state geologist, observed that "if there were no Yosemite, the Hetch Hetchy would be fairly entitled to a world-wide fame."

For years after its "discovery," Hetch Hetchy, like the rest of Yosemite's backcountry outside the lands protected in the Yosemite Grant, was

The Hetch Hetchy Valley before construction of the O'Shaughnessy Dam. COURTESY OF THE YOSEMITE NATIONAL PARK ARCHIVES, MUSEUM, AND LIBRARY

subject to the claims and depredations of private interests; miners could prospect there, and sheepherders could run flocks across the meadows like lawn mowers. When Hetch Hetchy was included within Yosemite National Park, the idea was that the protections that went along with being part of a national park—meaning the land could not be "used" for anything but the pleasure of all the nation's people, for all time—would be conferred upon Hetch Hetchy just as they were upon the rest of the park. This would not come to pass.

"IMPERIAL" SAN FRANCISCO

The City by the Bay had been burgeoning since the gold rush. With the population boom came the need for infrastructure, and infrastructure required natural resources. San Francisco got those resources—wood, stone, metal, water—wherever it could find them, and the Sierra Nevada was a supermarket for all of the above. Environmental concerns weren't even on the radar as the city embraced the industrial era. Timber was clear-cut from slopes around Lake Tahoe, in the Sierra foothills, throughout the Coast Ranges. Gold-country mountainsides were blasted with water and explosives to get at the minerals within, or quarried for the stone and aggregate to build roads and structures. Streams great and small were dammed, redirected, and sequestered to accommodate development and agriculture.

The city's barons had made their fortunes in a number of ways, through mining, railroading, shipping, banking, and merchandising. To bolster their power and their pocketbooks, some also formed water companies, claimed water rights around the Bay Area and beyond, and then sold the water to the region's growing municipalities. The Spring Valley Water Company controlled the supply for San Francisco and some neighboring communities, and used its stranglehold to wring money out of the city and manipulate its politics. San Francisco's leaders, as time went on, bucked against the monopoly.

It wasn't just about the money. The city also wanted to be the crux of the West Coast, the center of commerce and politics on the Pacific. Water was critical to that goal, and so San Francisco, led by an ambitious mayor named James Phelan, looked to secure its own, independent water supply.

The mighty rivers flowing out of the Sierra Nevada were the logical and likely sources, and they also could provide another commodity San Francisco badly needed to grow: hydroelectric power.

Mayor Phelan, along with the commission established to evaluate San Francisco's options, zeroed in on the Tuolumne River and a dam in the Hetch Hetchy Valley in the late nineteenth century. The city had been offered water rights on the river years before, but determined the costs were too high. In 1890, Phelan and the city decided that the time was right. It didn't matter that the Upper Tuolumne and Hetch Hetchy had, that very year, been protected within the boundaries of the newly designated Yosemite National Park.

DAM HETCH HETCHY

> *In these ravaging money-mad days monopolizing San Francisco capitalists are now doing their best to destroy the Yosemite Park, the most wonderful of all our great mountain national parks. Beginning on the Tuolumne side, they are trying with a lot of sinful ingenuity to get the Government's permission to dam and destroy the Hetch-Hetchy Valley for a reservoir, simply that comparatively private gain may be made out of universal public loss, while of course the Sierra Club is doing all it can to save the valley.*
>
> —John Muir, from the *Sierra Club Bulletin*,
> Vol. VI, No. 4; January 1908

Mayor Phelan would first file for water rights in the Hetch Hetchy Valley in 1901. That petition—filed in Phelan's name, not in San Francisco's—was quashed by Secretary of the Interior Ethan Hitchcock in 1903. In his denial, Hitchcock cited the fact that the valley was within the boundaries of Yosemite National Park.

Phelan was undeterred, and would apply again for the right-of-way to build a dam in 1905. Meanwhile, the Sierra Club, recognizing the threat, amped up its efforts to tamp San Francisco down. Muir and the club's secretary, attorney William Colby, spearheaded the fight. In addition to campaigning via articles in the *Sierra Club Bulletin* and editorials in newspapers and magazines, Colby would also organize a Sierra Club High Trip into Hetch Hetchy in 1904, one of several staged in those years to raise awareness of just what was at stake.

Secretary Hitchock denied San Francisco's second dam petition for the same reason as the first: Hetch Hetchy was protected as national park property. But then circumstances were horribly and abruptly altered. On April 18, 1906, the San Andreas Fault ruptured, and San Francisco quaked, crumbled, then burst into flame. More than five hundred square blocks were consumed in the massive blaze that followed the temblor, and between earthquake and fire, upward of three thousand lives were lost (there's no exact record of the death toll). The quake destroyed water lines in the city, which meant firefighters had nothing with which to douse the flames. The fire spread virtually uninhibited for three days. In the aftermath, the city fathers took stock. Significantly, in addition to acknowledging the failure of the infrastructure, administrators also focused on water supply, and that led them back to Hetch Hetchy.

San Francisco took its Hetch Hetchy lobby to Washington in 1907, where its arguments gained traction with sympathetic officials, including Gifford Pinchot, head of the two-year-old US Forest Service. While Pinchot understood that America's new forest reserves, including Yosemite, were intended to be preserved, he also believed the mandate dictated they could be put to their "highest and best use." Logging, grazing, and dam-building on these public lands were not anathema to the forest service chief. This contradicted the strict preservationist arguments of the Sierra Club and Muir, who believed national parks and monuments like Yosemite should remain untouched, as God intended.

But Muir demonstrated pragmatism in the face of San Francisco's argument. The naturalist proposed to his friend, President Teddy Roosevelt, that the government give the city rights to develop Lake Eleanor, also within the park boundaries, as a reservoir. Though that too represented a sacrifice, Muir hoped it would be sufficient to move the target off the Hetch Hetchy Valley. The aging naturalist understood the difficult decision Roosevelt faced. He acknowledges, in the *Sierra Club Bulletin*, that "the President, recognizing the need of beauty as well as bread and water in the life of the nation, far from favoring the destruction of any of our country's natural wonder parks and temples, is trying amid a host of other cares to save them all."

Roosevelt wasn't the only one grappling with a new paradigm. The ideas of conservation and preservation were still in the crucible, and Hetch Hetchy was a ball of glass taking shape in the flame. Conflict even flared within the Sierra Club, with some members voting in favor of the dam. Among Sierra Club proponents was member Marsden Manson, city engineer for San Francisco, who would go on to make the appeal to the Department of the Interior to reopen the city's petition for the water rights in Hetch Hetchy in 1908. While the Sierra Club membership would ultimately, and overwhelmingly, vote to formally oppose the dam, individuals like Manson did—and still do—find themselves stepping in what Kenneth Brower calls "ethical potholes" on certain issues.

With changes in the political sphere came changes in Hetch Hetchy's status. Secretary of the Interior Hitchcock, who had established himself in the preservation camp by turning down San Francisco's dam plan twice, was succeeded by James Garfield, who would fall into the conservation (Pinchot) camp. In approving San Francisco's final appeal in 1908, Garfield maintained that the city should not fall victim to the bloodsucking water companies of the era, and that its beleaguered citizens should have access to the purest water possible, essentially free, from the Tuolumne. The Hetch Hetchy project would also satisfy other claims to water rights on the river, including those of irrigation districts in the Central Valley towns of Modesto and Turlock.

"Furthermore," Garfield wrote, "the reservoir will not destroy Hetch Hetchy. It will scarcely affect the canyon walls. It will not reach the foot of the various falls which descend from the sides of the canyon. The prime change will be that, instead of a beautiful but somewhat unusable 'meadow' floor, the valley will be a lake of rare beauty."

Secretary Garfield's ruling essentially sealed Hetch Hetchy's fate, but the political wrangling would persist for years. One of the most significant arguments against congressional approval of the dam plan was the idea that San Francisco's water and power needs could be met by damming

Lake Eleanor alone, or by creating a reservoir on another river, such as the Mokelumne—or even by damming the Tuolumne downstream of Hetch Hetchy and outside of Yosemite National Park.

As votes on legislation to authorize the Hetch Hetchy project loomed in the two houses of Congress, debate raged in the media. Public sentiment outside of San Francisco ran strongly against the dam proposal. An outpouring of protest appeared in more than two hundred newspaper editorials, and some were collected in *Bulletin No. 2* of the National Committee for the Preservation of the Yosemite National Park, a spin-off of the Sierra Club. The press pulled no punches. An editorial sampling:

> *"The act creating the Yosemite National Park sets forth the importance and duty of reserving these wonders 'in their original state,' and the world has a moral right to demand that this purpose shall be adhered to. The 'beautiful lake' theory deceives nobody. An artificial lake and dam are not a substitute for the unique beauty of the valley."*
>
> —New York Times

> *"The whole project has a bad leak. Let San Francisco go elsewhere for her hot water; engineers agree that other sources are available."*
>
> —The Cleveland Plain Dealer

> *"If Uncle Sam means to give away this priceless valley of Hetch-Hetchy to become a reservoir for one city, does he propose to do something equally handsome for all the other cities of the nation?"*
>
> —Philadelphia Telegraph

> *"Entirely apart from whether this plan is not a piece of vandalism, the cool effrontery of San Francisco is sufficient for unmitigated condemnation. And considering the water is not needed so much for domestic supply as it is wanted for the promotion of manufacturing concerns, no good reason whatever exists why San Francisco should not buy its water man-fashion."*
>
> —New Bedford Standard

Wapama Falls. PHOTO: HERBERT W. GLEASON. COURTESY OF THE SIERRA CLUB.

San Francisco's media lashed back in editorials and cartoons, disparaging the Sierra Club and portraying the dam opponents as "unmanly and impractical," according to Kenneth Brower. The son of the Sierra Club's first executive director, David Brower, goes on to note that "[t]his characterization of tree huggers as elitist and effete is a tradition still with us."

Regardless the outcry, the bill known as the Raker Act—introduced by California congressman John Raker, who would also pen the legislation that led to the establishment of Lassen Volcanic National Park in 1916—would get the go-ahead from both houses of Congress. President Woodrow Wilson signed the act into law on December 19, 1913. San Francisco was authorized to dam Hetch Hetchy.

RAISING THE DAM

Everything about the Hetch Hetchy project is extraordinary.

First, there's the Tuolumne itself. The river begins as two forks in Yosemite's high country, "rushing cool and clear from its many snow and ice-fountains on the crest of the Sierra Nevada," in the words of John Muir. One of the forks begins on Mount Lyell, at 13,120 feet the highest point in Yosemite National Park. The other fork flows from the snow slopes of Mount Dana, a neighboring 13,000-foot peak. The Dana and Lyell Forks meet in Tuolumne Meadows, then launch down the river's Grand Canyon, a place of storied waterfalls and uncrowded wilderness. The canyon run ends in Hetch Hetchy.

Then there's the O'Shaughnessy Dam, named for the engineer who oversaw its construction, Michael O'Shaughnessy. More than 660,000 cubic yards of concrete were used to create the original arch-gravity dam, with some of the aggregate mined from the Hetch Hetchy Valley itself. It now towers 312 feet above the riverbed, the original structure having been raised 85 feet in 1938 to provide more storage. The original dam took nearly ten years to build, and cost the city of San Francisco about $100 million.

The reservoir itself, when full, impounds more than 360,000 acre-feet of water (each acre-foot covers one acre, one foot deep), about 117 billion gallons. Because the water level fluctuates depending on downstream water and hydroelectric demands, the reservoir's length and depth vary, but the lake behind the dam can stretch nine miles back into the canyon, cover nearly two thousand acres, and achieve a maximum depth of about three hundred feet. Because hard Sierra granite underlays the reservoir and the river that feeds it, silting is not a major problem, nor is surface evaporation, given the narrowness of the valley. To maintain the fishery downstream, shafts of the Tuolumne are jettisoned from outlets below the dam, arcing flumes of white water that ricochet off the canyon walls before resuming a raucous, if diminished, flow through the Poopenaut Valley and on to the confluence with the San Joaquin River.

Construction of O'Shaughnessy Dam commenced in 1914. Development of a dam on Lake Eleanor was supposed to come first, and, according to engineer Marsden Manson's 1908 appeal for permission to create the reservoir, building in Hetch Hetchy was only to begin "when the needs of the city and county of San Francisco and adjacent cities may require such further development." That's not exactly how it went. The dam on Lake Eleanor, and the Early Intake Powerhouse located twelve miles downstream from the dam site, were employed to generate electricity and power for the construction site at Hetch Hetchy. No one waited for a downstream need to be demonstrated.

The Utah Construction Company was employed to build the dam. In the years that followed, the Hetch Hetchy Valley would be clear-cut, and cofferdams and diversion tunnels built to funnel the Tuolumne away from the dam construction site. The Hetch Hetchy Railroad connected the valley to the outside world via Groveland, ferrying men and materials sixty-eight miles on a year-round schedule to accommodate the construction. The construction camp erected in the Hetch Hetchy Valley housed the four hundred to five hundred men who worked on the project (sixty-eight people would lose their lives in the dam's raising). Roadways were also laid down, with San Francisco promising to build one around the lake to accommodate tourism. This was never completed.

Engineering and construction of the dam were just part of the Hetch Hetchy project. Tunnels and pipelines (penstock) to move the water toward its ultimate destination were also built, taking another ten years or so to complete. The system is gravity-fed: The Mountain, Canyon, and Coast Range tunnels were bored through the mountainous regions along the descent to San Francisco, and pipeline was laid across the relative flats in the Central Valley. Pipelines form a rough circle around and across the southernmost lobe of San Francisco Bay, feeding into the Pulgas Tunnel. The system ends at the Pulgas Water Temple, with the Tuolumne feeding three reservoirs that lie in the San Andreas Fault rift zone just south of San Francisco.

San Franciscans would finally taste the Tuolumne in 1934. Today, about 2.5 million people in the Bay Area receive water from the Hetch Hetchy system; San Francisco also "wholesales" the Tuolumne to neighboring towns and cities. More than 260 million gallons of water arrive in the bay region every day, delivered via more than 280 miles of pipeline, sixty miles of tunnel, and eleven reservoirs, according to the Bay Area Water Supply and Conservation Agency. Although there are water treatment plants along the line, the water from Hetch Hetchy is so pure it has received a filtration avoidance from the US Environmental Protection Agency, which means filtration is not required.

Three hydroelectric facilities were built along the system in the foothills of the Sierra. The Kirkwood Powerhouse is highest on the Tuolumne, with the Moccasin Powerhouse farther down the line, and the Holm Powerhouse located below the Cherry Lake and Lake Eleanor reservoirs. These power plants, driven by water and gravity, generate 1.6 billion kilowatt-hours of power each year.

Construction of the dam did not completely destroy the scenic and environmental values of the Tuolumne. Eighty-three miles of the river below the O'Shaughnessy Dam and above the Don Pedro Reservoir have been designated wild and scenic. (The Merced River is so designated as well, within the boundaries of Yosemite National Park.) The South and Middle Forks of the Tuolumne are also born in Yosemite, and join the main river outside the park, as does the Clavey River and the North Fork Tuolumne River. The wild and scenic designation ends as the river flows into the massive Don Pedro Reservoir, another link in San Francisco's Sierra-fed water supply system.

And above the surface of the Hetch Hetchy reservoir itself, the domes, waterfalls, and granite faces are still impressive. The floor of the valley is at 3,783 feet above sea level, with the summit of Hetch Hetchy Dome,

The Hetch Hetchy Reservoir. PHOTO: PENN CHOURRÉ

on the north side, at 6,174 feet, and Kolana Rock, on the south side, reaching 5,774 feet. The two most impressive falls on the north side— Wapama, which flows year-round, and Tueeulala, which is seasonal— plummet about 1,000 feet from summit to reservoir. Farther upstream, as the Hetch Hetchy narrows, Rancheria Falls cascade into the basin. The valley straddles the ecotone, or transitional zone, between the montane and foothills biological communities, enabling a diverse floral community to thrive above the high waterline. All the landforms above that waterline are protected as wilderness.

But recreation at the lake is prohibited. To maintain the purity of the water, no swimming or boating is permitted. A scenic trail crosses the dam and follows the shoreline past Tueeulala Fall to Wapama Falls. The link to Yosemite's backcountry via the Grand Canyon of the Tuolumne was cut by rockfall below Rancheria Falls in 2014, so it's a relatively short, though scenic, out-and-back affair. Once the trail is restored, it will be easier for hikers to link Hetch Hetchy to Tuolumne Meadows. But the promise made by San Francisco during the dam debates—that Hetch Hetchy as a lake would provide the same recreational opportunities that Hetch Hetchy as a valley had—was empty. San Francisco never followed through.

RESTORE HETCH HETCHY

When the Raker Act was signed into law in 1913, John Muir knew the stately trees that shaded the banks of the Tuolumne in Hetch Hetchy would be clear-cut, and that the wildflower gardens he loved would be trampled in survey and construction, and then they'd be drowned. That knowledge, many say, broke the old naturalist's heart; he would die in the waning days of 1914. Robert Underwood Johnson, publisher of *Century* magazine and Muir's longtime friend, wrote this after Muir's death: "The best monument to [Muir] would be a successful movement, even at this late day, to save the Hetch Hetchy Valley from appropriation for commercial purposes. His death was hasted by his grief at this unbelievable calamity, and I should be recreant to his memory if I did not call special attention to his crowning public service in endeavoring to prevent the disaster. The Government owes him penance at his tomb."

The damage was done, but good things would come from the battle over Hetch Hetchy. Perhaps most significantly, Congress would pass the Organic Act in 1916, establishing the National Park Service. The new entity was charged with promoting and regulating national parks, monuments, and reservations, "to conserve the scenery and the natural and historic objects and the wild life therein and to provide for the enjoyment of the same in such manner and by such means as will leave them unimpaired for the enjoyment of future generations." Muir, called the "Father of the National Park Service," would have approved. Even so, the national park mandate, and the parks themselves, continue to come under fire from private interests.

The battle for Hetch Hetchy is also widely acknowledged to have ushered in the modern environmental movement, which has steadily gained strength in the decades since the reservoir was created. The Wilderness Act, signed into law in 1964, the Clean Water Act, passed in 1972, and the Endangered Species Act, signed in 1973, are all outgrowths of the awareness that Hetch Hetchy raised.

Additionally, the loss galvanized the Sierra Club. Hetch Hetchy was not the last dam battle the environmental group engaged in; it also successfully opposed proposals to create reservoirs in Dinosaur National Monument, near Kings Canyon, in Glacier National Park, and elsewhere. More significantly, the club has never abandoned the idea that Hetch Hetchy could be reclaimed. It produced films and literature throughout the middle of the twentieth century advocating the removal of the dam. In 1999, the club and other conservation organizations launched a spin-off group, Restore Hetch Hetchy, which seeks to "undo this great American mistake" by restoring the valley, while not denying San Francisco its ability to take water from the Tuolumne River. The city would just divert it, and store it, outside Yosemite National Park.

Environmental groups are not the only ones to call for the reclamation of Hetch Hetchy. In 1987, Donald Hodel, secretary of the interior under Ronald Reagan, came out with a proposal to remove O'Shaughnessy Dam and drain the reservoir. Studies conducted in conjunction with the Hodel proposal looked at the impacts on water and power supplies, but not on environmental impacts or public use. Based on those criteria, Hodel determined that the idea of demolition and restoration was worthy of further study.

Hodel's plan, predictably, was opposed by politicians from the City by the Bay. Then mayor Dianne Feinstein would declare the Hetch Hetchy Reservoir the city's "birthright." The plan went nowhere.

Since the Hodel proposal, restoration of Hetch Hetchy has been caught up in a report war. Studies by the Environmental Defense Fund, Restore Hetch Hetchy, the University of California, Davis, the California Department of Water Resources under governor Arnold Schwarzenegger, and others have pointed to the economic, engineering, and environmental feasibility of taking down the dam, providing replacement water and power to San Francisco from alternative sources, and reclaiming Hetch Hetchy. San Francisco's public utility commission has fired back with statements in opposition, claiming, among other things, that the quality of Hetch Hetchy water can't be replicated, sourced as it is from protected wilderness. Creating a reservoir downstream on the Tuolumne, as many of the restoration proposals suggest, would expose consumers to runoff from agriculture, mine tailings, and even effluent from wastewater plants, the public utility commission asserts.

The press has also weighed in on the restoration issue. In 2004, following up on some of the reporting done by the environmental groups and others, the *Sacramento Bee* published a series of editorials advocating removal of the dam and restoration of the valley. The paper and its editorial writer, Tom Philp, won a Pulitzer Prize for the series in 2005.

California's Resource Agency published a Hetch Hetchy Restoration Study in 2006, which consolidated the recommendations of twenty years' worth of documents published in the report wars. The upshot: All of the stakeholders would need to find consensus if the valley were to be restored: the political machine in the city of San Francisco, the National Park Service, state and federal departments of reclamation, and the public. The idea that the valley could be restored has, as the Resource Agency report states, "no fatal flaws," but the costs—financial, environmental, and social—have yet to be ironed out.

The questions are many. Would demolition cost $2 billion, or $10 billion, or more? Should the dam be removed completely? Partially? Left in place, with the reservoir drained behind it? How should be valley be reclaimed in the wake of the draining of the reservoir? What public uses should be allowed? Where would replacement water for the San Francisco system be stored? How would water rights be affected? How could archaeological and historic sites be reclaimed? Do O'Shaughnessy Dam and the Hetch Hetchy water system comprise a historic site in and of themselves? How should the wishes of Native tribes, such as the Tuolumne Band of Me-Wuk and the Southern Sierra Miwuk Nation, be incorporated into a restoration plan?

With those questions yet unanswered, and consensus still distant, the story of Hetch Hetchy continues to unfold.

THE TEMPLES OF THE TUOLUMNE

The long transit of the Tuolumne River from Hetch Hetchy to San Francisco ends on Cañada Road in Woodside, in the San Andreas Fault rift valley. The outlet is behind the Pulgas Water Temple, erected in the Beaux Arts style to commemorate completion of the Hetch Hetchy water system. "I give waters in the wilderness and rivers in the desert, to give drink to my people," is etched into the frieze below the temple's cap. A long reflecting pool fronts the structure, surrounded by lawn that stays brilliantly green long after the dry season has bleached the surrounding hillsides blond.

The river pools again behind the temple, now contained in the Crystal Springs Reservoir, which sprawls below the forested ridges of the Coast Range. Behind the temple the plumbing is utilitarian, a long shaft of concrete feeding into the dark blue waters of the reservoir. From here, the Tuolumne is sucked into lines that feed the faucets of San Francisco.

A short trail leads from Cañada Road to the water temple. You can sip the Sierra from a drinking fountain in the parking lot.

There is paradox in this place. John Muir celebrated the Hetch Hetchy Valley as "one of nature's rarest and most precious mountain temples." The Pulgas Water Temple celebrates the ingenuity of humankind. One temple is a battlefield, the other is obscure, but they are linked in the clearest, purest way. The Tuolumne flows through them both.

Images of Yosemite

THESE DAYS, EVERYONE'S A PHOTOGRAPHER. DEVICES CARRIED IN THE pockets of Yosemite National Park visitors transmit images of waterfalls, domes, giant sequoias, and the great peaks along the Sierra crest worldwide. They project visions of the mountains with an ease that the photographers and artists of the past could only have dreamed of.

It's not hard to imagine, however, that yesterday's artists didn't long for something like this thing called the World Wide Web as they carefully packed their bulky cameras and fragile glass plates, or boxes of paint and canvases, onto beasts of burden for the long journey by rough wagon road from Yosemite back to civilization. How much easier it would have been to settle back in the grass along the banks of the Merced, compose an image, and press a button to send it off into the world.

No such luck. Photography, sketching, and painting in the wilderness was, in the nineteenth century, a cumbersome task. Thankfully, Yosemite's early artists braved the hardships. Without them, preservation of the Valley and the Mariposa Grove might never have come to pass.

It could be no other way. The granite monuments and cathedrals of the Yosemite Valley and its backcountry can't help but inspire the pencil, brush, and lens of even the most ordinary visual artist. But the skilled professionals who brought power to the pictures would inspire preservation of the park, then vividly illustrate, in their unique ways, the reasons why that preservation was so important.

ART MAKES THE PARK

The first commercial artist in the park was part of the tourist group that included Yosemite's earliest promoter, magazine publisher James Hutchings. On his 1855 tour of Yosemite Valley, Hutchings brought along sketch

Yosemite Falls, by Thomas Ayres. COURTESY OF THE YOSEMITE NATIONAL PARK ARCHIVES, MUSEUM, AND LIBRARY

artist Thomas Ayres to illustrate the region's reportedly unparalleled vistas, including Yosemite Falls, and the gateway to the Valley. Ayres's work would accompany Hutchings's written descriptions in *Hutchings' Illustrated California Magazine*.

Ayres, a New Jersey native described as an "artist-argonaut" by one writer, had come to California early in the gold rush years. He didn't strike it rich in the goldfields, but he was able to make a living sketching landscapes and scenes from mining camps. His talents served Yosemite well, but for all that his sketches captured the majesty he saw with astonishing accuracy, Ayres, by one account, found the task daunting. To show the size of the place—Yosemite Falls as the highest in America, the massive sheer face of Half Dome, the gateway from Inspiration Point—he struggled to illustrate scale. By incorporating distance and perspective he was beautifully successful, but in the end viewers on the East Coast didn't believe what they were seeing. He even described Yosemite in words, in an article published in the *Daily Alta California*. But Ayres's images, along with the words of Hutchings, would need backup.

The answer, Hutchings decided, lay in photography, where artistic license could not be accused of stretching the truth and authenticity would not come into question. A photographer could establish Yosemite's credibility. But it would be expensive. Landscape photographers in the mid-1800s required specialized equipment that was cumbersome, heavy, and costly. Photographs were taken on glass plates, which were first treated with chemicals in a makeshift, on-site darkroom (a tent), exposed using a bulky camera mounted on a tripod, then rushed back to the darkroom for another bath in chemical developers. The "wet plates" were both fragile and heavy, as was the camera itself. Historians estimate that each of the plates composed by Charles L. Weed, who was hired by Hutchings to take the first photographs of the Valley and the Mariposa Grove in 1859, weighed a pound and a half, and that the camera weighed forty pounds.

Like Ayres, Weed focused on iconic sights, including Yosemite Falls, and like Ayres, his work was used by Hutchings to promote the scenic wonders of the future park. He got the job done.

Carleton Watkins, a contemporary of Weed's, also had a solid reputation as a professional photographer when he traveled to Yosemite in 1861.

Mirror: The Three Brothers, by Carleton Watkins. DIGITAL IMAGE COURTESY OF THE GETTY'S OPEN CONTENT PROGRAM

Another Easterner who'd headed west in the gold rush, Watkins found work in Sacramento ferrying supplies to the mines before abandoning the capital city for San Francisco to work as a professional photographer. On his first trip to the Valley, Watkins was armed with a "mammoth-plate camera, which used 18-by-22-inch glass plate negatives, and a stereoscopic camera," according to one biography.

In advocating preservation of the Yosemite Valley and the Mariposa Grove of Big Trees as a public park, Watkins's images, along with those of Ayres and Weed, were presented by Captain Israel Raymond to the US senator from California, John Conness. Raymond is quoted as admonishing the politician to "[p]reserve the park and look at these!" Conness would, in turn, present the images to Congress and President Abraham Lincoln in support of his bill to create public reserves in the Valley and the grove. Duly impressed, the powers that be signed the Yosemite Grant Act into law. The sights that had enchanted the nation in pictures could now be enjoyed in real life for posterity.

Watkins would return to Yosemite following the passage of the act, hired as the official photographer of the California Geological Survey by its chief, Josiah Whitney. His images illustrate Whitney's *The Yosemite Guide-Book*, which documents the boundary-defining survey. Watching Watkins at work, surveyor William Brewer would observe in his journal: "The difficulty of access and the expense deter most of those who would wish to visit this place, yet [the] photographer packed in his apparatus on mules and took a series of the finest photographs I have ever seen." Mount Watkins would be named for the photographer.

Watkins went on to capture more memorable images on journeys in the Sierra mining camps, into Oregon, and in Alaska. He would win awards for his work, and establish studios of his own in San Francisco. Weed, too, would return to work in Yosemite and publish his images later in the 1860s. Ayres, sadly, would go down with a ship that foundered outside San Francisco Bay in 1858.

ART IN THE PARK: THE EARLY DAYS
Even as the works of Ayres, Weed, and Watkins were being parlayed into parkland in the nation's capitol, the premier landscape artists of the

era were making the long trek into Yosemite, setting up their easels, and going to work.

Albert Bierstadt was among those pioneering artists, and his dreamy paintings of the Valley, bathed in mist and soft light, were much admired by viewers back east. The dreaminess was in the style of the Hudson River School, but one Yosemite interpretive ranger notes that Bierstadt may have simply captured what he saw, a Valley softened by the smoke of ground fires, which were common in those days.

Thomas Moran, better known for documenting the landscapes of what was then the Yellowstone territory, also created splendid images of Yosemite after a visit in 1872. His body of work, including field sketches in watercolor and pencil from Yellowstone, were instrumental in convincing Congress and President Ulysses S. Grant to create Yellowstone National Park in 1872. Moran's images of other stunning wild places in the West, such as the Grand Canyon, were part of the campaign that resulted in establishment of the National Park Service in 1916.

Landscape painter Thomas Hill first visited Yosemite in 1865. Considered one of Yosemite's premier artists, his landscapes have the same ethereal, romantic quality as Bierstadt's; Hill was also influenced by the Hudson River School. Born in England, Hill emigrated to the States as a teenager and studied at the Pennsylvania Academy of Fine Arts. He also studied in Paris, and then ran a studio on the East Coast before heading west and settling in California in 1861. He split his time between San Francisco and Wawona; his studio, on the grounds of the Wawona Hotel, was built by John Washburn, who married one of Hill's daughters. In the late 1880s, having separated from his wife, he became Wawona's "resident artist," and, according to park literature, made a good living there, selling more than 160 paintings in three years.

Photographers also thrived on the visual bounty of the newborn Yosemite Grant, despite the hardships associated with the work. Stereography, or stereo photography, was one way early photographers could add depth to the images they captured in the park. Using a dual-lens camera, which was much less onerous to transport than a plate camera, pictures taken side by side were viewed through a special device to create the desired effect. The introduction of dry-plate exposures in the late 1870s,

Looking down the Yosemite Valley from the Sylvan Bar, by Eadweard Muybridge.
DIGITAL IMAGE COURTESY OF THE GETTY'S OPEN CONTENT PROGRAM

and of cameras that used film (the genius of George Eastman, inventor of the Kodak camera), would lighten the load considerably.

But before these improvements and techniques were widely employed, English-born Eadweard Muybridge, yet another frontiersman turned photographer, arrived in Yosemite in 1867 armed with a mammoth camera and even bigger glass plates. His images stand apart not only for their quality, but also because Muybridge, who adopted the pseudonym "Helios," was a bit of a wild man, given to extremes to capture a scene. He climbed farther into the backcountry and, so the story goes, not only had himself lowered over the Valley rim so he could get the perfect shot, but also chopped down trees that obscured views. Later, Muybridge would make history with his freeze-frame images of human and animal locomotion. Another claim to fame: Muybridge shot and killed his wife's lover, but would win acquittal when jurors deemed the act a justifiable homicide.

George Fiske, a protégé of Carleton Watkins's and an apprentice under Charles Weed, was able to enjoy improvements in technology during his long tenure as a photographer in Yosemite. Born in New Hampshire, Fiske traveled to the park several times in the 1870s, then overwintered in the Valley at the end of the decade, capturing spectacular winter scenes. He and his family moved to Yosemite permanently in 1882, securing a lease from the commission that oversaw administration of the Yosemite Grant. The commissioners, including guardian Galen Clark, recognized the value of his work, which documents the Valley's evolution over three decades.

Fiske's images, which dominate historic photographs and portraits from the grant era, are widely admired, not only by the casual observer, but also by fellow photographers. Reflecting on the sad fact that many of Fiske's negatives were destroyed when his Valley home burned in 1904, and the rest in another fire in 1943, Ansel Adams is quoted as saying, "If that hadn't happened, Fiske could have been revealed today, I firmly believe, as a top photographer, a top interpretive photographer. I really

This George Fiske photograph shows a saddle train on the trail, with Nevada Fall as backdrop. COURTESY OF THE NATIONAL PARK SERVICE HISTORIC PHOTOGRAPH COLLECTION.

can't get excited at Watkins and Muybridge—I do get excited at Fiske. I think he had the better eye."

Fiske's studio was one of many that populated the Valley floor under the auspices of the Yosemite Grant. Maps and histories document a number of artists' studios in the villages—Best's, Fagersteen's, Boysen's, D. J. Foley's (a print shop), Pillsbury's, and Jorgensen's, kept by Chris Jorgensen, one of Yosemite's best-known landscape artists. However, being an artist/leaseholder in the grant was not always easy. Historian Hank Johnston recounts the experience of painter Charles Dorman Robinson, who spent a decade traveling to and from Yosemite before securing a lease in 1885. He was ousted two years later by the guardian, Walter Dennison, who appropriated Robinson's studio for his own purposes. Robinson's suit against the commission and the guardian, alleging malfeasance, was dismissed, but engendered criticism of the commission within the press.

ART IN THE PARK: INTO THE PRESENT

The heyday of artists occupying studios within the park tapered off after the Yosemite Grant was folded into Yosemite National Park in 1906, and the National Park Service took over management in 1916. That didn't stop the work, however. In fact, in 1916, one of the most influential and renowned photographers Yosemite would ever know made his first visit to the Valley.

Ansel Adams remains Yosemite's premier artist into modern times. His images, no matter the subject, are bold, brooding, and sublime, pairing light and shadow both as opposites and in partnership. He was a master of the filter, a master in black-and-white, a master of composition. Though earlier Yosemite photographers excelled in depicting the park's beauty and, more importantly, helped document the park's evolution, they all fall short of the artistic ideal established by Adams. Given modern equipment and techniques, would Watkins or Fiske have been able to capture the imaginations of generations as Adams has been able to do? Perhaps. But it's a moot point. Adams took the prize and, even in death, continues to hold it.

Adams, a native of San Francisco, was a teenager when he became infatuated with Yosemite. His life was built within and around the park, from his years working as a guide based out of the Sierra Club's LeConte Memorial Lodge to his marriage to Virginia Best, the daughter of landscape painter Harry C. Best, who operated Best's Studio under a Yosemite Grant lease. Of the dozen or so studios that cropped up in the park over the grant years, Best's is the survivor, now called the Ansel Adams Gallery and operated by the renowned photographer's family.

In those early years Adams was steeped in the concepts of conservation as well as the wonders of nature. His involvement with the Sierra Club extended long past his service at the LeConte lodge; he'd lead and photograph High Trips starting in the 1920s, and later join the club's board of directors. His advocacy for preservation grew more strident as the number of visitors to Yosemite swelled, demonstrated both in his ongoing campaign to limit that visitation and in his efforts to curtail commercialization of the park. He, like Yosemite's premier wordsmith, John Muir, would lobby politicians and in the press to scale back National Park Service policies that threatened to destroy the natural values of Yosemite. Adams was, for example, vehemently opposed to the NPS Mission 66 program plan that resulted in improvements to the Tioga Road, but only by blasting away eye-catching, glacier-polished granite near Tenaya Lake. Among his quotes: "With Yosemite, we have one of the most extraordinary places on earth, but Yosemite possesses a 'fatal beauty,' which invites self-destruction unless we make a strenuous effort to control visitation and use."

Adams's portrayal of Yosemite is pure, and that's how he thought the park should be. He lived to see the worst of Yosemite's commercialization—the crowds, the noise, the pollution—but the pictures that helped motivate those tourists to visit, even as they sat in their smoking cars and piled onto overcrowded trails, were the ones Adams captured of the park's unspoiled beauty. *Monolith, the Face of Half Dome* is the classic; as art, it is as iconic as Half Dome is in nature. The conundrum of the artist/conservationist could have been fraught with hypocrisy, but Adams was faithful in his belief that, in terms of managing Yosemite National Park, no balance could be struck unless the weights were stacked on the side of nature, not on the side of the tourist and concessionaire.

Adams died in 1984, too early to see the gradual swing back toward preservation that has been manifest in Yosemite in recent history. He, like

Muir, would doubtless still be appalled at the crowds and commercialism in the park, but it has been trimmed, both through policy and due to the nature of the place.

Adams's legacy includes a peak on the Sierra crest named in his honor, and a generation of modern photographers who, when they look at the world, see it, at least in part, through Adams's lens. It's not just about how he captured the scene; it's also about how he took into consideration the care and maintenance of the natural world. Case in point: Galen Rowell, another Yosemite photographer whose pictures are sublime. Rowell also helped expose, and end, a controversial park practice that resulted in the destruction and senseless disposal of problem bears. Rowell publicized photographs of the bodies of the dead bears, which had been dumped off the side of a park highway.

Artists working in other media—oils, watercolor, woodcuts, pencil—continued to turn out stunning works in the twentieth century. Documenting the natural world took on an educational focus as well. Walter Sedoriak created detailed images of the flowers of the park for publication; Della Taylor Hoss created stunning linoleum block prints of the park's trees to illustrate Mary Curry Tresidder's *The Trees of Yosemite*, published by the Yosemite Natural History Association in 1931. Swedish-born Gunnar Widforss composed light-splashed landscapes in Yosemite and in other national parks, notably the Grand Canyon. Photographer Dana Morgenson, a Yosemite Park and Curry Co. employee who was famous for his wildflower studies, led "Camera Walks" in the Valley in the mid-twentieth century.

Japanese-born artist Chiura Obata, who first traveled to Yosemite in 1927, would impose an evocative and illuminating clarity on Yosemite's landscapes—vivid colors, simple lines, and hard edges. He was schooled in Japan, and emigrated to San Francisco in 1902, where he would garner attention for his sketches of the aftermath of the San Francisco earthquake and fire. These, coupled with his landscapes of Yosemite and elsewhere, would propel Obata into a professorship at the University of California, Berkeley, in the 1930s. That post would not preclude hardship: Obata was interned with other Japanese Americans in Topaz, Utah, during World War II. Ever the teacher, Obata established an art school in the internment camp, encouraging students to find solace in nature.

Half Dome and the Yosemite High Country from Sentinel Dome, by Carleton Watkins. DIGITAL IMAGE COURTESY OF THE GETTY'S OPEN CONTENT PROGRAM

Despite the overwhelming peace that emanates from images of Yosemite like Obata's, acquiring new perspectives meant Yosemite's artists and photographers had to be, in some instances, mountaineers, or at least packers. Though most, whether professional or amateur, managed to get in and out of the backcountry without harm, the tragic story of painter, photographer, and writer Stephen Lyman illustrates just how dangerous the desire for the right light, or the right angle, could be. Lyman, just thirty-eight, and already recognized for his fine paintings, was a John Muir enthusiast and followed in his mountaineering footsteps, finding inspiration in the wilderness. He died among the Cathedral Rocks, in a chute facing the Three Brothers, in 1996, having taken a fall while trying to take photographs in a storm.

Lyman's circumstance is unusual, but brings into sharper focus the skills and risks taken by the photographers and artists who had come before.

Art in the Park: Going Forward

Every year, a new class of artists and photographers discovers the natural beauty of Yosemite and exposes it in novel ways. The Yosemite Museum regularly curates exhibitions from its collections. Yosemite Renaissance, a nonprofit organization, supports contemporary painters, photographers, multimedia artists, and sculptors with an exhibit that's taken place, on and off, since 1985. Students are encouraged to enter their Yosemite-inspired works of art and poetry in what has become, in recent years, an annual contest. In the Ansel Adams Gallery, the images of the masters are on display, and prints are available for purchase. The tradition of art in the park, from the mysterious pictographs in the Grand Canyon of the Tuolumne to the stunning black-and-white photographs of Alan Ross, is in Yosemite for the viewing.

Meanwhile, in the meadows and on the mountaintops, a hundred hands are slipping into pockets, retrieving the device, and capturing the image that, with luck or the magic of Photoshop, will become a master-piece of memory worthy of a frame and a spot on the study wall.

The Climbers

THE SHEER WALLS OF EL CAPITAN ARE, FOR MOST MORTALS, SIMPLY A wonder. Snap a picture; lay back in the meadow and capture their massiveness in the mind's eye; carry their promise of adventure forever there.

For others, this granite monolith and its neighbors—Half Dome, Washington Column, Sentinel Rock, the Royal Arches, Cathedral Rocks—are big walls to climb.

Yosemite Valley's long and colorful climbing history is chock-full of characters. That's the thing about rock climbers: Their personalities—and egos—tend to be as big as the walls they climb. For the everyman, that might not be such a good thing. For a big-wall climber, a touch of madness and unassailable self-confidence are prerequisites.

Yosemite's climbing history is evolutionary as well, as the brightest lights of one era built a foundation for the accomplishments of the next. One has to wonder, however, what those early mountaineers, surveying the stony peaks of the Sierra crest in wool and sturdy boots, would have thought of today's climber, spider-walking up an impossible face in skintight booties, sleeping in bivouacs hanging thousands of feet off the ground, perhaps capping off the climb by leaping off the summit in a flying squirrel suit.

Yet if John Muir met John Long, chances are the two would find their passions for the aeries of Yosemite's big walls have the same wellspring: a love of wild places and of limitless adventure.

MOUNTAINEERS

First ascents are badges of honor among today's Yosemite's climbers, who meticulously record who did what first on which rock, wall, or peak. Not so for Yosemite's Native people, the Ahwahneechee. Theirs was an oral tradition, so documenting a climb—a first, second, or hundredth ascent of any of the summits in the Yosemite Valley or the high country—happened in a story told at a feast, in a roundhouse, around an evening campfire. But the first people of Yosemite blazed trails linking the isolated valley to tribal villages in Hetch Hetchy and Wawona, and to the Mono Lake Paiute across the Sierra crest, on the east side of the range. It seems reasonable that one Ahwahneechee, or many, stood on the mountaintops long before men with pens arrived.

For the region's first American mountaineers, reaching a summit or forging a new path up a seemingly inaccessible canyon was a means to a scientific end. They delighted in their ascents, but first they were geologists, botanists, biologists, and mapmakers, exploring a strange new world. Still, modern-day rock jocks have much respect for routes established long ago; check any Yosemite climbing guidebook, and you'll find the authors have noted first ascents by men who were not "climbers" by avocation.

The first documented ascent in what is now Yosemite National Park was accomplished as part of the California Geological Survey of the High Sierra. The team that surveyed the Yosemite Valley and high country in 1864 included state geologist Josiah Whitney, botanist William Brewer, and topographer Charles Hoffmann. These men climbed all over the region, mapping, measuring, and describing the flora and fauna they encountered. After surveying in the Valley, the men moved into the backcountry and made the first recorded ascent of a peak on the Sierra crest, which they named Mount Hoffmann.

"It commanded a sublime view," Brewer wrote in his journal, words any Yosemite climber, even one who simply mounts a rock after driving to Glacier Point, understands in the bone. "Perhaps over fifty peaks are in sight which are over twelve thousand feet, the highest rising over thirteen thousand feet. Many of these are mere pinnacles of granite, streaked with snow, abounding in enormous precipices . . . it is sublimely grand—its desolation is its great feature . . . The scene is one to be remembered for a lifetime."

That team, later joined by Clarence King, who would become the first director of the US Geological Survey, summited and named a number of the Sierra's highest peaks in the seasons that followed. King and colleagues made a circuit of high points around the Valley rim in 1864, linking El Capitan, Eagle Peak, North Dome, Mount Watkins, Sentinel Dome, and others. In the tradition of the time, the surveyors often named geographic high points for important explorers, scholars, and scientists, or for themselves: Mount Brewer, Mount Dana (for James Dana, whom Brewer calls "the most eminent of *American* geologists"), Mount Lyell (for Charles Lyell, "the most eminent of *English* geologists"), and, of course, Mount Whitney, at 14,505 feet the highest peak in the contiguous states, named for the survey's leader.

As Yosemite fledged into parkhood, some of its most prominent personalities emerged as mountaineers and canyoneers of extraordinary talent and bravery—though the focus was still on scientific, artistic, or conservationist endeavors. Among his many wild tramps, John Muir logged first ascents of Cathedral Peak and Mount Ritter in the future park's high country, and scaled the cliffs alongside Yosemite Falls to check out the moon from behind the water. Geologist Joseph LeConte, University of California, Berkeley professor and Sierra Club cofounder, pioneered routes to the bases of big walls that are still used by climbers today. Yosemite guardian and respected mountaineer Galen Clark blazed trails of discovery into the park's deep woods and steep canyons.

These mountaineers weren't seeking summits for the sake of summits themselves, but that would follow on naturally. And the most obvious target for such an effort was Yosemite's most iconic high point, Half Dome. The California Geological Survey team and others had pronounced Half Dome "entirely inaccessible," but that would prove false in short order.

John Conway, who envisioned and built some of the most spectacular trails in Yosemite, first attempted to climb the dome in the early 1870s. With either one son, or a team of sons, Conway drilled and fixed a series of "bolts" on the dome, sending the younger ones up the rock to fix a rope as they ascended. (In an article describing his own successful ascent, Muir called Conway's companions "a flock of small boys who climb smooth rocks like lizards.") Conway eventually retreated, however, leaving the summit for another man to conquer.

That was George Anderson, called by Muir an "indomitable Scotchman," who reached the summit on October 12, 1875. Accounts of Anderson's success, and the attempts that preceded it, include harbingers of techniques used to conquer other "unconquerable" faces in Yosemite more than a century later. Hoping to increase his purchase on the slick granite, Anderson reportedly tried wrapping his feet in cloth smeared with sticky pitch; it proved a bit too sticky, but the idea is reminiscent of the modern sticky-rubber climbing shoe. Anderson also furthered Conway's technique of using bolts to secure a rope for safety and provide aid on a climb. He inched his way to the summit, drilling holes in the rock and placing iron eyebolts, a precursor to the "ladder" that assists modern climbers on Half Dome today.

Half Dome is a summit of magical proportions; an ascent can, and has, changed the trajectories of lives. So it's no surprise that tourists followed swiftly on Anderson's ascent. To accommodate the onslaught, the Sierra Club first replaced the ropeline with metal cables and footrests in 1919. That cable system is still used today, with summiteers queuing up at the base of the final pitch. In the summer season, thousands of visitors apply for permits to climb Half Dome, and hundreds make the ascent every day. Few are climbers; in fact, according to rangers, a good number aren't even hikers. But the dome's allure—its promise of a grand reward for an inward and outward journey that challenges both body and psyche—is a magnet for even the nascent mountaineer.

BIG WALLS

As the decades passed and Yosemite matured as a park and playground, climbing became sport. The challenges were classified: At the most basic level, Class 1 routes are hikes, with no special equipment or skills required. The earliest mountaineers, like King and Brewer, made Class 3 or 4 ascents, requiring scrambling or simple climbing techniques, with the use of a rope for protection optional.

Among the first to explore the technical challenges offered by the Valley's steeper canyons and faces were the park's assistant postmaster, Charles Michael, and his wife, Enid, who would become Yosemite's first female ranger-naturalist. The Michaels made ascents of such difficulty and with such exposure that modern-day climbers are impressed, especially given the rudimentary equipment available in the Michaels' day. Other key practitioners of more technical climbing in the early part of the twentieth century included James Hutchinson and Joseph N. LeConte ("Little Joe"), son of the Sierra Club cofounder.

In 1931, climbing in Yosemite took on a new dimension. Robert Underhill brought the concepts of advanced ropework from Europe to a group of young Sierra Club climbers in California, a group that included such luminaries as Glen Dawson, Jules Eichorn, Richard Leonard, Bestor Robinson, and Raffi Bedayn. The development of "pitoncraft," which anchored ropes to rock, enabled climbers to contemplate, and then conquer, routes that hadn't been possible before. Making use of the techniques Underhill introduced, the focus turned to the big walls, spires, and pinnacles. These specialized tools and techniques were prerequisite to ascending such faces, as a fall would be fatal. Class 5 climbing had arrived.

Mountaineers from the Sierra Club—including David Brower, who would become president of the conservation organization—made a number of Class 5 first ascents in Yosemite in the 1930s and the early 1940s. John Salathé, a Swiss-born blacksmith in his mid-forties who would have a profound impact on the Valley's climbing culture, also arrived in Yosemite in the 1940s. His introduction to mountaineering was through the Sierra Club. He wasn't well physically, and perhaps not mentally, either; the story goes he believed his wife was poisoning him, and an angel convinced him to become a vegetarian. But like legendary mountaineers who had come before, Salathé found both health and well-being in Yosemite's high places.

Taking to the sport with passion, Salathé and partners pioneered several iconic routes, including a first ascent of the Lost Arrow, the distinctive formation adjacent to Yosemite Falls, and the classic Steck-Salathé Route on Sentinel Rock. He also applied his blacksmithing skills to the problem of the iron climbing pitons used to protect routes, which would bend when hammered into Yosemite's hard granite. Back at his shop in the Bay Area, Salathé forged a hard steel piton, developing a "Lost Arrow" of a design still manufactured by Black Diamond Equipment Ltd., a premier outdoor retailer.

THE GOLDEN AGE

It is 3,300 feet high, a plain, severely simple, glacier-sculptured face of granite, the end of one of the most compact and enduring of the mountain ridges, unrivaled in height and breadth and flawless strength.
—JOHN MUIR ON EL CAPITAN, FROM *THE YOSEMITE*

John Salathé also mentored the climbers who would dominate the Valley climbing scene from 1955 to the early 1970s, dubbed the "golden age" of Yosemite big-wall climbing. Driven and eccentric, this generation pioneered routes up nearly every cliff. What had been off-limits was now within reach.

The drama of the climbing culture took on a new narrative in this era as well, as two powerhouses competed to conquer Yosemite's most iconic climbs: The Nose of El Capitan, and the sheer, tear-stained face of Half Dome.

Warren Harding, who would be called the "iron man of Yosemite" as well as "Batso," arrived in the Valley in 1952. By all accounts he was a wild man, arguably Yosemite's first dedicated climbing bum. He was a hard drinker and, as he would tell one interviewer, his climbing technique "was to thrash his way up a route any way he could, and finesse be damned."

Flip the coin and there was Royal Robbins, a serious young climber with a strict aesthetic. He did his share of partying in Yosemite's Camp 4, but when it came to climbing, Robbins epitomized finesse. Clean climbing was his cause and mantra.

In this case, opposites did not attract. Robbins and Harding would wage an epic war of one-upmanship on the Valley's big walls.

Robbins took the first prize in 1957, as he and his team made the first ascent of the coveted Regular Northwest Face of Half Dome. It was a groundbreaking climb, the men spending five days on the two-thousand-foot wall, hauling all their gear and water. It was also a climb that Harding had attempted, and failed, a couple of years earlier.

But Harding would capture the second prize: the first ascent of The Nose of El Capitan. This was, again, an "impossible" climb, ascending more than three thousand vertical feet along the distinctive, bulging prow

Nothing is impossible, even if it's perpendicular. COURTESY OF GEORGE MEYERS

of the monolith. It took him a couple of years to accomplish, ascending to a high point, fixing ropes, descending to rest and recoup, climbing the ropes to the previous high point, and continuing up to the next. After forty-five days of climbing, and drilling 125 bolts to protect the line, Harding and his team made the summit in November 1958.

The first ascent of The Nose was considered a "turning point" in the climbing world, opening every big wall in the Valley to assault using Harding's "siege" and bolt techniques. Robbins's next play was to follow on by climbing The Nose in only seven days. Again, the gauntlet was thrown.

Harding and partner Dean Caldwell answered by climbing El Cap's Dawn Wall, another seemingly unclimbable expanse of sheer granite. It took them the better part of a month to make the climb, and they endured several days trapped on the wall by storms. They also placed three hundred bolts along the route.

Robbins followed on with a vengeance. Placing that many bolts went against his "clean climbing" ethics, which would become dominant in the climbing universe as time went on. So, in his assault on the Dawn Wall, he "chopped" the bolts from the line. For a couple of pitches, anyway—the climber would later acknowledge that Harding had established a premier route. Robbins and partner Don Lauria used the rest of the bolts placed by the wild man to complete their ascent.

The single-mindedness of Harding and Robbins and the luminaries who climbed with and after them—Tom Frost, Chuck Pratt, Yvon Chouinard, Dean Caldwell, Layton Kor, Steve Roper, and Bev Johnson, all of whom made significant contributions to the climbing world—shaped the future of the sport in Yosemite. But they did more than just open the floodgates on the impossible. The climbers of the Golden Age also established a culture. And that culture created a home for "hobos who would climb forever" in Yosemite's Camp 4.

THE STONEMASTERS

Yosemite is no wilderness, and the climber must share the relatively small space with thousands of other visitors. It is still possible for the

imaginative climber to find a quiet day, alone with the cliffs and the swallows. Nighttime is a different story; Yosemite is remembered among the regulars for its boring nights as much as its exciting days. The options are limited: the lodge and its bar, restaurant and lounge, or back to camp. Books help, but it is difficult to find a place to read. Solution? There is no solution, but you will have lots of company.
—FROM *YOSEMITE CLIMBS*, BY GEORGE MEYERS

Climbers often describe themselves in reverential terms: bold, visionary, brilliant. People on the outside often use other words, typically some variation on insane and/or suicidal.

But one label comes from both directions: *outlaw*.

The self-styled "Stonemasters" who occupied Camp 4 and monopolized Yosemite's big walls in the 1970s epitomized this persona. Youth, the cultural revolution of the 1960s, supreme athleticism, and a complete disregard for boundaries propelled this generation of climbers to new competitive heights.

The climbers of the Golden Age—considered outlaws themselves—had knocked down the monster first ascents, so the Stonemasters set new goals. To start, they went for speed. The Nose of El Cap had been climbed, but no one had climbed it in a day, so in 1975 three of Yosemite's big wall best—Jim Bridwell, John Long, and Billy Westbay—took the summit in a flashy fifteen hours.

The Stonemasters also transformed Royal Robbins's clean climbing ethic into a new style called free climbing. Where Warren Harding and others had used equipment to assist in their ascents (bolts, ascenders, ladders; hence, the moniker "aid climbing"), the Stonemasters employed only their hands and feet on the granite, using ropes solely to protect themselves in the event of a fall, and developing gear that could be "cleaned" from cracks once a pitch had been topped.

This generation of climbers also logged their share of gnarly first ascents. Sure, El Cap, Half Dome, Washington Column, and the other big walls *had* been climbed, but Stonemasters Bridwell, Long, John Bachar, Ron Kauk, Tobin Sorenson, and their contemporaries established new routes that pushed climbers' physical limits. Recall the Class 5 rating:

Within that class, the difficulty of a climb can be broken down even further, with 5.0 being the easiest, and 5.15 (at least, for the present), being the most difficult. To be even more exact, routes are given an "a," "b," "c," or "d" rating, with "a" being easier than "d." The Nose route is rated 5.8, with aid. A free climb of The Nose, as first accomplished by Stonemaster Lynn Hill, is rated 5.13.

The new, hard routes of the 1970s were enabled by the development of clean climbing tools including "nuts" (not climbers themselves, despite the interesting double entendre). These hi-tech gadgets, some called hexes, others Friends, were used to protect big-wall climbers in the event of a fall, and were easily cleaned as a team ascended, leaving no trace. Chalk that could sop up sweat on fingertips and palms, and shoes that fit like slippers, with soles of sticky rubber, both helped solidify a free climber's grip on the granite.

Another Stonemaster innovation: guidebooks. They directed climbers to specific routes and illustrated the details of what might be encountered on any given line. Steve Roper was the first to publish a guidebook to Yosemite climbing in 1970. This was followed by guidebooks compiled by George Meyers and Don Reid. Graphic illustrations, called topos, were detailed and keyed, with approaches, corners, bolts, sections of face climbing and crack climbing, liebacks, off-widths, dihedrals, flakes, arêtes, belay stations, rappel lines, and other arcane but necessary information meticulously documented.

The Stonemasters also essentially turned Camp 4 into a giant party. In the documentary film *Valley Uprising: Yosemite's Rock Climbing Revolution*, Hill laughs as she calls her cohorts "stoned masters." The film (and other sources) also chronicle the chemically enhanced brilliance of legendary climber Jim Bridwell. Bridwell, nicknamed "The Bird," bridged the gap between the era of Robbins, Harding, and Chouinard and that of the Stonemasters, and terrorized the teams he climbed with as he tripped up "impossible" lines high on psychedelics.

The Stonemasters worked in teams to accomplish their goals. They trained together, sculpting godlike physiques; partied together, sometimes to the distress of other Yosemite visitors; and planned together, plotting new lines and helping each other prepare gear and supplies for

Climbing isn't all tension and brawn, even if you are on belay. COURTESY OF
GEORGE MEYERS

bold ascents. Status was earned by doing, and gender was not a barrier: Hill and the other accomplished female climbers of the era were not relegated to a "hen party," à la the Sierra Club's 1951 *Wilderness Handbook*. As they finessed the most difficult climbs, they were welcomed into the tribe.

It was a little harder for newcomers to the Valley to assimilate, as the competitive spirit that drove Harding and Robbins was alive and well among the Stonemasters. In a *Rock and Ice* magazine article, writer Duane Raleigh describes how now-legendary climbers Bachar and Kauk "worked together to crack Yosemite's rigid caste system, strengthening themselves on a regimen of 100 push-ups and pull-ups a day. For Bachar, being recognized by peers such as Bridwell and John Long (who intimidated Bachar with his massive physique and bodacious bullshitting) was everything."

Irreverence was, for the Stonemaster, the norm and the expectation. The staid names previously given to climbs, which had been descriptive or honored the first ascenders (think The Nose, or Steck-Salathé on Sentinel Rock) became bizarre. "Butterballs" and "Butterfingers"; "Piton Pooper" and "Lunatic Fringe"; "Basket Case" and "Mother's Lament"; "Jesus Built My Hotrod." The climbers also blatantly disregarded authority (as had climbers in the Golden Age), defying park rangers who tried to rein in the bad behavior that could, and did, upset Yosemite's paying tourists. Conflicts with the National Park Service were commonplace. But there was also cooperation: Climbers worked with Yosemite's search-and-rescue teams on a number of occasions.

While it sounds like an athletic bacchanalia, the era was not without somber moments and loss. Climbing is, no matter the planning, the gear, and the physical and mental strength of the participant, a dangerous undertaking. Mess up on El Cap or any other big wall or big mountain, and a climber will shatter on talus thousands of feet below. The literature for Yosemite alone documents hundreds of climbing and mountaineering casualties. The Stonemasters would lose and mourn comrades like Sorensen and Bachar, who both died on solo climbs outside Yosemite. But that risk hasn't, and won't, scare a climber off a big wall.

Lodestar Lightning

In the closing days of 1976, a plane went down in Yosemite's high country, plunging into freezing Lower Merced Pass Lake. The crash and its aftermath would fundamentally alter the hobo nature of the Stonemaster climbing culture.

Hikers first alerted the park to the crash, having spotted a wing tipped on edge between two trees, according to the authors of *Off the Wall: Death in Yosemite*. Park rangers, along with agents from US Customs and the Drug Enforcement Agency, would determine that the plane's two occupants, both killed in the crash, had been smuggling thousands of pounds of marijuana from Mexico.

Federal officials were able to confiscate tons of contraband from the submerged plane and keep the cargo secret for a time, but winter weather forced them to abandon salvage efforts. Word of the downed plane and its illicit cargo, however, had leaked into the climbing community. Snow, ice, and wind be damned: The "stoned masters" were coming. A modern gold rush was on.

The dope was nicely packaged in 140-pound bales, but icebound (as were the bodies of the pilot and his partner). This impediment was overcome by climbers armed with axes, elbow grease, and the occasional chain saw. As the ice receded, the climbers fished for bales from the shoreline. They carried it down to Camp 4 in backpacks, dried it out, and lit it up. Seeing as it had been soaked in gas and oil leaked from the plane after the crash, the weed that became known as "Airplane" and "Lodestar Lightning" *really* lit up.

The Valley's wall rats also realized they could sell the contraband, netting funds that would buy them a whole lot of new gear, and cars, and trips to other climbing hot spots. A *Mountain Gazette* article from the time called it the "Big Score." And the outlaws didn't bother to hide what they'd collected: An enterprising entrepreneur created T-shirts that read, "I got mine at Lower Merced Pass Lake."

It didn't take long for the authorities to catch on and close off access to the lake. In the early spring of 1977, armed rangers were airlifted into the basin to enforce the law, scattering the miscreants who were still looking for salable, smokable goods. The crash site was placed under guard

Some flakes must be trusted. COURTESY OF GEORGE MEYERS

until the bales of pot that had not been appropriated were confiscated by authorities, and the bodies of the pilot and passenger were recovered. By summer, there was nothing left at the site.

The influx of money from Lodestar Lightning roughly corresponded with the mainstreaming of rock climbing and the Stonemasters' descent from dominance. In the early 1980s, the stars of Yosemite rock became stars in the wider world, with climbers like John Bachar, Lynn Hill, and Ron Kauk doing commercials and appearing on television. Magazines like *Rock and Ice* and *Climbing* published stories of big wall and big mountain adventure written by Yosemite climbers. Others, like John Long, would launch careers as authors, publishing books like *How to Rock Climb!*, a classic how-to guide to the sport.

The Stonemasters also encountered a divisive bolt controversy, reminiscent of the conflict that dominated Yosemite's Golden Age. In this drama John Bachar was the purist, chopping the bolts set into stone by the new breed dubbed "sport climbers," who trained in gyms, practiced on boulders, and competed on artificial walls for money, endorsements, and fame. Bachar would chop bolts from routes in the fashion of Royal Robbins, and this, as it had decades before, would cause friction within the tribe. The Stonemasters splintered, and then moved on. The torch was passed.

CRANKING IT UP

Free soloing is climbing at its purest: no aid, no team, no rope or gear. Just a climber and the rock. A natural extension of the free-climbing revolution initiated by the Stonemasters, the free solo would become a hallmark of the next generation of Yosemite climbers, including John Bachar and Peter Croft.

Of the Stonemasters, Bachar was the premier free soloist, playing on his strength and talent to knock off a number of first free ascents in Yosemite and elsewhere before his fatal accident. Amping up the level of the free solo sets apart the brightest names among Yosemite's current crop of climbers. The self-styled Stone Monkeys have reached the next level of extreme by climbing the big walls free and fast, by linking two or three big-wall climbs in a single day, and by adding a new dimension to the idea of "rappel": the BASE jump.

The climber who wrote the book on speed climbing—literally—is Hans Florine. The fastest lizard on the wall, Florine and his partners, over a span of about twenty years, squeezed a one-day ascent of The Nose on El Cap from fifteen hours to just more than two hours. To say the man knows that face better than anyone alive is also not an exaggeration: In 2015 he completed his one-hundredth ascent of The Nose.

Florine's partner for the current speed climbing record is Alex Honnold, the new kid and, at least for now, Yosemite's most daring free soloist. Honnold is, by all accounts, a phenomenon. His daring and elegant free solo climbs of Yosemite's biggest walls, including Half Dome, and his endurance—he linked ascents of Mount Watkins, Half Dome, and El Cap, known as Yosemite's Triple Crown, in a single day—have earned him both celebrity and the respect of his peers.

Another pair of new-generation climbers would swing into the media spotlight in January 2015. Tommy Caldwell and Kevin Jorgeson completed the first free ascent of the Dawn Wall on El Capitan in what has been hailed as "the most difficult ascent in the history of rock climbing." This "featureless" face, with several pitches rated 5.13, and an overall rating of 5.14, had been the setting for the epic battle of style waged by Warren Harding and Royal Robbins in the 1960s. It took the pair nineteen days to complete, and they did most of the climbing in twilight, when the rock was cool and easier to stick to.

But the most extreme of Yosemite's Stone Monkeys was Dean Potter—free soloist, big-wall climber, slackliner, BASE jumper, and, in the finest Valley tradition, outlaw.

Potter demonstrated the ubiquitous traits of the Yosemite climber—speed, daring, and endurance—in the "usual" ways, holding the El Cap speed record for a time, and completing a trail run/climb to the top of Half Dome, then back to the Valley floor, in just more than two hours.

But Potter added two additional elements to the mix. Slacklining, or highlining, is essentially tightrope walking—only in Yosemite, the tightrope is fixed thousands of feet off the ground, slung across, for example, the gap at the top of Yosemite Falls. Potter walked that line, walked a line to the Lost Arrow Spire, and walked other lines in other exotic locales.

He was also a BASE jumper and wingsuit flyer.

BASE jumping, defined as parachuting from a fixed structure like a bridge, antenna, span, or earth, can be construed as a "natural" extension of climbing—the ultimate rappel, the quickest and most outrageous way to descend after topping out on a big wall. One problem: It's not legal in national parks.

Yosemite saw its first BASE jump in 1966, and given the setting, the Valley walls quickly became a popular destination for jumpers. Among the most colorful practitioners of the sport, according to Steve Roper, was stuntman Rick Sylvester, a climber known for his "ski/parachute leaps" off El Capitan.

But serious issues quickly surfaced, the most obvious being the fact that things could go spectacularly wrong on a BASE jump. Rescuing injured jumpers or retrieving bodies was an expensive and dangerous undertaking in Yosemite, and elsewhere. National Park Service officials questioned whether BASE jumping in any national park was compatible with the park mandate. In the case of Yosemite, for instance, shouldn't visitors crane their necks to appreciate the splendor of the walls and spires rather than to watch daredevils hurl themselves off the bitter edge and then (hopefully) glide to a safe landing? Ultimately, parachuting for sport (whether as part of a skydive or a BASE jump) was prohibited within all national parks.

Park officials in Yosemite did attempt a compromise, agreeing to "host" jumpers using a mechanism in the ban that allowed them to issue permits for parachutes, like it did for hang gliders. But the risks and costs were still deemed too high, and BASE jumping was banned.

The prohibition provoked protest among the sport's aficionados. But the risks were inescapable, as tragically illustrated by the death of Jan Davis, a stuntwoman with a BASE jump off Angel Falls in Venezuela on her résumé. In 1999, Davis joined colleagues in a leap off El Cap as part of an organized protest against the BASE jumping ban. A crowd assembled to watch the team of jumpers/protestors, and rangers were there to arrest and fine each upon landing. Her colleagues landed safely, but Davis's equipment failed and she died on impact. Instead of proving how safe the sport was, she had demonstrated how fatal it could be.

Still, BASE jumpers and wingsuit flyers snuck up onto Yosemite's rim to launch and fly, risking arrest for the thrill. That's what Potter and partner Graham Hunt did in May 2015. Wearing wingsuits, they leapt off Taft Point into Yosemite's gaping mouth, and were swallowed. Despite the fact that what they did was unlawful, the grief following their deaths was palpable, in the park and beyond. Dean Potter's remarkable accomplishments on Yosemite's big walls, and his tenure as one of its greatest mountaineers, were now legacy.

THE CENTER OF THE EARTH

Climbers call Yosemite the "center of the Earth." But they have become part of that center, have become integral to the park's identity. They are specks on massive faces; they stand bleary-eyed in the deli line, wrapped in blankets while waiting for their morning jolt; they stride along the Valley's trails carrying packs that bulge with ropes and chime with gear. Everyone recognizes them; everyone stands in awe of them. After all, we grew up with them: the brother taunting us from the highest limb of a redwood tree; the niece swinging from the chandelier over the dining room table; the best friend running pell-mell down the dock and launching off the end, chest out, head thrown back, arms akimbo. We knew they were going to grow up and do radical things; things we wouldn't dare attempt, but that we admired fundamentally.

In Yosemite, we bestow on the mountaineer our inner daredevil, and through that climber or trekker, we take on the epic and come out on top. Their adventure, like the park itself, is ours.

Sculpting Yosemite:
Tales of Glaciers and Waterfalls

THE AHWAHNEECHEE TOLD FANTASTICAL STORIES OF HOW YOSEMITE'S granite monoliths came to be. El Capitan rose magically beneath a pair of sleeping cubs. The measuring worm that inched up the sheer walls to rescue the cubs then stretched across the Valley and back, weakening the walls and creating rockslides. To punish a bickering wife and husband for their wickedness, the spirits of the Valley turned them to stone; she became Half Dome, and he, North Dome.

The scientific truth is no less fantastic. The natural forces that created the world's largest monolith and many of North America's highest waterfalls are nothing less than awesome. And the story is not limited to the technical, though the mechanics of faulting, glaciation, fracturing, and erosion are critical players. It's also the story of the men who studied Yosemite's geology and, like Tis-si-ack and her husband, argued over it.

THE BIOGRAPHY OF YOSEMITE'S GEOLOGY

The Sierra Nevada were born when two of the massive tectonic plates that make up the Earth's crust collided, a creative and destructive force that still crumples California today. The Pacific Plate met the North American Plate, upon which most of the state rides, and being denser than its continental mate, dove under in a process called subduction. There, in a cauldron about five miles under the surface, a massive block of granite was forged, about four hundred miles long, ten miles thick, and sixty miles wide.

The formation of the Sierra batholith took place about one hundred million years ago. In the millennia that followed, heat-powered tidal shifts in the Earth's mantle began to raise the bubble of rock. The mass slowly cooled and hardened as it was forced upward, solidifying into the distinctive, crystal-specked granite backbone of today's Sierra Nevada range.

As the Sierra were lifted, erosion worked on a layer of rock and soil two to five miles thick that had been deposited much earlier by the volcanoes that composed an ancestral range. Shapes and aspects were slowly but relentlessly altered, landscapes molded and remodeled by the grinding of the plates and the work of water and ice. Then, about twenty-five million years ago, faults broke along the east side of the range, which began to tilt westward. That tilting, combined with the uplift, steepened the slopes and caused rivers to flow more swiftly and carve more aggressively. The flows washed rich sediments down into the sea, which in that epoch reached the foot of the mountains. As the shape-shifting continued, this oceanic trench would drain and evolve into California's fertile Central Valley.

Despite the consequence of a misstep, Glacier Point's ice-carved Overhanging Rock has invited awe and playfulness for more than a century, as this photo by George Fiske attests. COURTESY OF THE YOSEMITE NATIONAL PARK ARCHIVES, MUSEUM, AND LIBRARY

The crest of the Sierra approached its present height about three million years ago, with the tallest peaks piercing fourteen thousand feet. At the same time, the climate began to change. The ice ages began, a cycling through periods of glaciation and warming. The last glaciation in the Sierra, which commenced about one hundred thousand years ago, was augmented by a confluence of astronomical configurations—the tilt of the planet, the shape of its orbit around the sun, a wobble. Known as the Milankovitch oscillation cycles, these are predictable, and result in terrestrial climate cycles that translate to roughly one hundred thousand years of cold followed by ten thousand years of warmth. Interestingly, the last ice age ended about ten thousand years ago

Snow and ice, made ferocious by altitude and gravity, became erosive on a massive scale during the ice ages. Glaciers—great "rivers" of ice that flow and ebb—filled valleys throughout the mountains that had been previously carved by unfrozen waterways, rounding their distinctive V shapes to U shapes. In that way, ice fields remodeled the Yosemite and Hetch Hetchy Valleys, grinding their floors flat and steepening their granite sidewalls.

It took two million years for the glaciers to sculpt Yosemite's distinctive features. It wasn't a onetime event; the ice sheets advanced and retreated over time, revising earthworks done previously with each pass. Rocks and gravel caught in the undersides of the floes scoured granite like "giant pieces of sandpaper," leaving some surfaces as polished and shiny as patent-leather shoes. The ice peeled away the other half of Half Dome, breaking the granite into jumbles and depositing the pieces elsewhere. It smoothed the slopes and summits of North Dome, Sentinel Dome, Liberty Cap, and the high points in Tuolumne Meadows. It randomly dropped boulders, called "erratics," on slopes and in future meadows. It sheered the walls and sharpened the rims in the future park's two signature valleys, preparing cliffs to host waterfalls once the ice receded for good.

In the last ice age, before the retreat ten thousand years ago, a mother glacier about two thousand feet thick squatted over the high country at Tuolumne Meadows. The tallest points of the present-day park, including Half Dome, Cathedral Peak, Mount Lyell, and Mount Dana, poked above the ice. They provided pockets where life could survive in a frozen world: Called *nunataks*, these "sky islands" offered sanctuary to unique flora and remarkable animals, such as the Lyell salamander, which survive into modern times. More than one hundred species of wildflowers, including cushion plants like sky pilot, can still be found on sky islands at the highest altitudes in the park.

As it receded, the mother glacier split into smaller glaciers, one finishing its work on the Grand Canyon of the Tuolumne River and the Hetch Hetchy Valley, another following the course of the Merced River down through Tenaya Canyon toward the Yosemite Valley. John Muir would posit that fingers of glacier—the Yosemite Creek, the Hoffman, the Tenaya, the South Lyell, and the Illilouette—"welded themselves together into the main Yosemite Glacier, which, grinding gradually deeper, swept down through the Valley." The little fingers combined into a masterful hand.

As the glaciers retreated from the Valley and side canyons, meltwater streams—the forks of the Tuolumne, the Merced, Yosemite Creek, Bridalveil Creek—settled back into their ancestral beds, and where they met cliffs, they became waterfalls all around. Lateral moraines, deposits of silt and stone that mark the boundaries of glacial flows, would eventually be buried by rockfall, though the terminal moraine is still exposed near the west end of the Valley, under the watchful eye of El Capitan. For a time

Measuring the Lyell glacier. PHOTO: R. H. ANDERSON. COURTESY OF THE YOSEMITE NATIONAL PARK ARCHIVES, MUSEUM, AND LIBRARY.

that terminal moraine corralled a lake within the Valley. Silt slowly filled what is known as Lake Yosemite, which stretched miles back into the canyon; that silt underlies the Valley floor today.

Glaciers persisted in Yosemite's high country and throughout the Sierra long after the last ice age ended, established in a subsequent "Little Ice Age," and preserved by frigid temperatures and consistent snowfall at altitude. Though the "living glacier" famously discovered by Muir in 1871 has melted away, a handful of small glaciers remain within the park boundaries, among them the Lyell, Dana, and McClure glaciers. The Lyell glacier, the second largest in the Sierra Nevada, has diminished by more than 50 percent since 1880, according to park literature. Whether because of global climate change or simply as part of a natural process, geologists expect that, within fifty to seventy-five years, the last of Yosemite's glaciers will have melted away.

While glaciation is no longer a major force for geologic change in Yosemite, plate tectonics are still at work. The Sierra Nevada continue to rise as the North American and Pacific Plates slip, grind, and subside. On the surface, another consequence of the Sierra's formative subduction process continues to express itself. Tremendous pressure, as well as tremendous heat, created the park's granite faces, and as that pressure slowly escapes, it cracks the stone. The cracks delight rock climbers, who follow them to the summits of big walls. In other cases those cracks become flakes, another enabling, if unnerving, feature on some Yosemite big-wall climbs. With alarming regularity chunks of the cliffs exfoliate, careening downslope and exploding on impact, creating the mounds of talus found at the bases of cliffs throughout the park. Though their causes are known—rainfall, earthquake, freeze and thaw—rockfalls occur with little or no warning, terrifying those who witness them.

The more staid and steady forces of erosion are also still at work in the park: wind and water. Relentless and nearly imperceptible by human measure, they continue to chip away, the old men of the mountains, patiently whittling at hard and shiny stones.

Big Theories on a Big Landscape

Not a peak, ridge, dome, cañon, yosemite, lake-basin, stream or forest will you see [in the Sierra] that does not in some way explain the past existence and modes of action of flowing, grinding, sculpturing, soil-making, scenery-making ice.

—John Muir in *The Yosemite*

The primary geologic forces behind the Yosemite Valley's brilliant architecture have long been deciphered, but when Americans first explored the region in the mid-nineteenth century, the provenance of the immense cliffs, waterfalls, and domes was a matter of study and conjecture.

Some of the most well-respected geologic minds of the era went to work on the question. Josiah Whitney, head of the newly formed California Geological Survey, posited that the Valley had been formed by a cataclysmic foundational collapse, a theory supported by his scholarship and reputation as a Harvard professor. John Muir was convinced otherwise. Though he never earned a traditional degree, he had studied geology while a young man at the University of Wisconsin, and was convinced that glaciers were responsible for the architecture of Yosemite. Both men came to their conclusions after long, long walks in the field. They examined and contemplated the same phenomena, but their ideas about how those phenomena came to be were markedly divergent.

Whitney explained his theory in *The Yosemite Guide-Book*, which records observations made by the California Geological Survey expeditions of the mid-1860s. "Most of the great cañons and valleys of the Sierra Nevada have resulted from aqueous denudation," he wrote, "and in no part of the world has this kind of work been done on a larger scale. The long-continued action of tremendous torrents of water, rushing with impetuous velocity down the slopes of the mountains, has excavated those immense gorges by which the chain of the Sierra Nevada is furrowed, on its western slope, to the depth of thousands of feet."

But this didn't account for the shape of the Yosemite Valley, given the "squarely cut" angles of its walls. Whitney considered a variety of mechanisms. He dismissed the idea of a fault splitting the Valley, as it was too wide, and one side didn't fit neatly into the other. And "folding," he determined, typically creates valleys parallel to the orientation of the range, not valleys running perpendicular, as did the Yosemite.

Finally, Whitney dismissed glaciers. "Much less can it be supposed that the peculiar form of the Yosemite is due to the erosive action of ice," he maintained, and then aimed a dart at those who subscribed to the glacial hypothesis: "A more absurd theory was never advanced, than that by which it was sought to ascribe to glaciers the sawing out of these vertical walls and the rounding of the domes."

His answer? "In other and more simple language, the bottom of the Valley sank down to an unknown depth, owing to its support being withdrawn from underneath, during some of those convulsive movements which must have attended the upheaval of so extensive and elevated a chain [as the Sierra Nevada]."

Whitney did not entirely dismiss the idea that glaciers played a role in the topography of the Valley and surrounding mountains. He and his colleagues, future US Geological Survey chief Clarence King among them, acknowledged evidence of glacial action on Yosemite's granite domes. In the context of the Valley, Whitney surmised that water had filled the void after the collapse of the floor, creating a vast lake. "The gradual desiccation of the whole country, the disappearance of the glaciers and the filling up of the abyss to nearly a level with the present outlet, where the Valley passes into a cañon of the usual form, have converted the lake into a valley with a river meandering through it," he wrote.

John Muir, arriving in the Yosemite not long after the geological survey team, saw things quite differently. He read the story of Yosemite's glacial epoch in the "granite pages" of the Valley's sheer walls and among the lake basins of the high country. Terminal moraines deposited throughout the region as the ice fields retreated and the telltale polish on the granite, which he had seen in other glaciated landscapes, were key to his analysis. He would call the "glacial pavements" of Yosemite's high country, such as those found around Tenaya Lake and Olmsted Point, "the most striking and attractive of the glacial phenomena."

Muir proposed his theory in an article published in the *New York Tribune* in 1871. In the piece—the first he would publish, titled "Yosemite

Glaciers"—he described his explorations in the canyons that led from the Valley into the high country: Yosemite Creek, Illilouette Canyon, the canyon of the mighty Merced. Each hosted a river of ice at one time, he asserted, which cut and buffed the rocks before pulling back and dying away.

"The great valley itself," he wrote, "together with all its domes and walls, was brought forth and fashioned by a grand combination of glaciers, acting in certain directions against granite of peculiar physical structure. All of the rocks and mountains and lakes and meadows of the whole upper Merced basin received their specific forms and carvings almost entirely from this same agency of ice."

Moreover, Muir would voice his opinion that "future investigation [would] uncover proofs of the existence in the earlier ages of Sierra Nevada ice, of vast glaciers which flowed to the very foot of the range."

Despite acknowledging signs of glaciation in the High Sierra, Whitney had no problem dismissing Muir's observations. And he wasn't the only one. Whitney, after all, had professorship and a government appointment to back him up. Consequently, Muir's "views were assailed, ridiculed, and belittled as the wild fantasies of an ignorant shepherd," wrote one historian of the response to Muir's article.

For his part, Muir expressed similar disdain for those who subscribed to Whitney's theory. In *The Yosemite*, Muir wrote about the massive Inyo earthquake in 1872. A fault on the east side of the Sierra, its epicenter near what is now Lone Pine, rent the earth in a temblor the US Geological Survey estimates had a magnitude of 7.4. For comparison, the infamous San Francisco earthquake of 1906, which destroyed much of the city, had a magnitude of 7.8. Muir, wild man that he was, rushed out to watch the aftermath, exploring the still-shifting rubble that cluttered the Valley floor after a rockfall and riding out aftershocks with more curiosity than fear.

Other residents of the Valley, however, were rattled by the aftershocks and fearful of another rockfall. Coming together near the Hutchings House, Muir teased a believer in Whitney's "tumble down and engulfment" theory that they were all witnessing "another Yosemite-making cataclysm, which would perhaps double the depth of the Valley by swallowing the floor, leaving the ends of the roads and trails dangling three or four thousand feet in the air." The earth shook following his comments, and the believer, he observed, became "awfully silent and solemn." Muir tried to reassure the man that the earthquakes were nothing more than Mother Nature "trotting us on her knee," but the other left the Valley until "poor, trembling Yosemite was settled."

Others weighed in on the debate as well. Yosemite guardian Galen Clark, though not a geologist, was a keen observer of the natural world. His theory of the Valley's formation incorporated elements of both cataclysm and glaciation. "In some period of the earth's existence, while its granite crust in that locality was in a semi-plastic condition, by some great subterranean force of gases or superheated steam, its surface was forced up in places, forming these great dome elevations," he wrote. "In some instances this force was sufficient to burst open the surface and make a complete blow-out, forming a great chasm with vertical sides. The bursting open of two, or more, of these great domes seems to have been the original agency in the formation of Yosemite Valley." The debris left after the blowout, he concluded, would have been carried from the Valley by the glaciers that followed on.

In spite of the criticism and competing theories, Muir persevered. He went to Alaska in 1879 as a member of the US Coast and Geodetic Survey, and began to compile evidence to support his then-radical ideas about the agency of glaciation on Yosemite's cliffs and domes. Future trips to Alaska, as well as to the glacier-sculpted mountains of Norway and Switzerland, would enable him to gather sufficient material to write about, and thus sway, some scientists of the day to his side.

But the controversy wouldn't be settled until after the deaths of both Whitney and Muir. In the early 1930s, according to Yosemite geologists Allen Glazner and Greg Stock, Francis Matthes of the US Geological Survey took on the task of settling the debate. Matthes's investigation, bolstered by modern scientific techniques, would validate Muir's glacial theory.

But debates continue, as new science reveals more information about how geologic forces shape landscapes, both in Yosemite and beyond. As Glazner and Stock note in *Geology Underfoot in Yosemite National Park*,

"In light of new findings, some of the old ideas about Yosemite's geologic history are being questioned, or even abandoned. Such is the nature of science. Yosemite National Park has long been a place where new ideas about geology have been forged, and that will no doubt continue long into the future."

Waterfalls and Firefalls

Waterfalls, five hundred to one or two thousand feet high, are so subordinated to the mighty cliffs over which they pour that they seem like wisps of smoke, gentle as floating clouds, though their voices fill the valley and make the rocks tremble.
—John Muir from *My First Summer in the Sierra*

Yosemite's Native people feared and avoided the waterfalls of the Valley. The spirits that abided in the mists could snatch people behind the veil, and so the Ahwahneechee steered clear. In one version of the legend of *Po-ho-no* (Bridalveil Fall), people who wandered too close could become victims of an "evil spirit with the breath of a fatal wind." *Cho-lok* (Yosemite Falls) was also haunted by dangerous spirits; in that legend, a maiden gathering water below the falls pulled snakes from the stream, and in the end, her entire village was blown into the pool at *Cho-lok*'s base by a malevolent wind.

Enchantment by Yosemite waterfall continues into modern times, but the spirit that moves most victims to their dooms these days is not the stuff of legend. It's the lure of the better photograph, coupled with a lack of respect for—or ignorance of—the forces of nature. The authors of *Off the Wall: Death in Yosemite* detail the missteps of dozens of people who've died after disregarding signs posted at Vernal Fall, Nevada Fall, and Yosemite Falls warning visitors to stay clear of the waterways. They were swept over the edge while trying to snap a better shot, fill a water bottle, or, sadly, trying to rescue another person who had fallen into the river or stream.

Power, danger, beauty, and topography are integral to the allure of Yosemite's waterfalls. When the rains come, or come springtime after a good snow year, every face in the Valley weeps. When fully charged, the falls are thunderous and commanding, as irresistible to the viewer as the watercourse is to the geologic forces that transform it.

Given the abruptness of the terrain within the park, waterfalls are found on most every stream. They have been significant drivers in every phase of Yosemite's history. They inform Ahwahneechee legends and helped to inspire President Lincoln's signature on the Yosemite Act. Hotels and camps were situated so that visitors could have the best views of the falls. The unique characteristics of each, and their changeability day to day and through the seasons, bring people back to the park year after year.

Yosemite Falls, the fifth tallest in North America, is the "heartbeat" of the Valley. When fed by snowmelt and spring rain, it leaps free of the cliff at its apex, plunging 1,430 feet into the Middle Cascades, which rumble 675 feet before fueling the final 320-foot drop of Lower Yosemite Fall. Travel but a quarter-mile down the creek from the base of the lower fall and Yosemite Creek goes quiet, rolling placidly down to meet the Merced.

The premier falls on the Merced—Nevada and Vernal—are the two flashiest steps on the river's glacier-carved Giant Staircase. Nevada Fall is the mightier of the two: When fully charged, it flies 594 feet from a chute at the top, "as if glad to escape into the open air," wrote John Muir in *The Yosemite*. "But before it reaches the bottom it is pulverized yet finer by impinging on a sloping portion of the cliff about half-way down, thus making it the whitest of all the falls in the Valley, and altogether one of the most wonderful in the world."

Vernal Fall is downstream from Nevada, a rectangular sheet of water 317 feet high. Muir called Vernal the mellowest of Yosemite's falls, "a staid, orderly, graceful, easy-going fall, proper and exact in every movement and gesture."

Tucked into a canyon east of Glacier Point, Illilouette Fall is as graceful as its name, feathering 370 feet into a narrow gorge. And Bridalveil, haunted or not, is Yosemite's greeter, a focal point in most every classic historic photograph and painting of the Valley's gateway. It's also Yosemite's most accessible fall, with a short paved path leading into the wind-whipped cloud at the base of Bridalveil Creek's 620-foot vault. "[I]t sways

Vernal Fall. PHOTO: TRACY SALCEDO

and sings in the wind, clad in gauzy, sun-sifted spray, half falling, half floating, it seems infinitely gentle and finite; but the hymns it sings tell the solemn fateful power hidden beneath its soft clothing," wrote Muir.

The rock-star waterfalls have an impressive backup band, filling a stage that reaches into the backcountry. The cascades in and above the Grand Canyon of the Tuolumne are secluded but churn in unusual ways, with Waterwheel Falls, for example, throwing up spinning arcs of water before continuing its descent. In Hetch Hetchy, Muir likened ephemeral Tueeulala Fall to the Bridalveil. Tueeulala's neighbor, Wapama Falls, thunders year round, shattered into rolling cascades and wet smoke before meeting the placid water of the reservoir. One of John Conway's torturous but artful trails climbs more than four miles along the cascades on Chilnualna Creek.

Yosemite Valley welcomes a slate of guest players each spring, ephemeral falls that light the shadow clefts. Ribbon Fall, called a hanging waterfall because the stream that feeds it was left hanging after the glaciers plowed through, is unbroken as it hurtles 1,612 feet just west of El Capitan. Sentinel Falls rocket down the stepped face west of Sentinel Rock. Staircase Falls step down across the wall below Glacier Point and above Curry Village. And Horsetail Fall, on El Capitan's east side, lights up like a lava flow for a couple of weeks in late February. Photographers lie in wait for the opportunity to catch the fleeting illumination, which only occurs at the confluence of adequate snowmelt and the perfect angle of the sun.

Though not easy to do, catching Horsetail Fall on display is as close as a modern visitor will get to viewing one of Yosemite's most famous, historic, man-made attractions, a "waterfall" of embers known as Firefall. Firefall flickered on and off during its hundred-year history, as permitted by commerce, policy, and war. But for those who saw it (and even those who wish they'd seen it), the memory of this one-of-a-kind display—a cascade of burning coals pushed off Glacier Point after dark, golden fire tumbling thousands of feet to the Valley floor—kindles awe and desire.

Firefall originated in the 1870s, when James McCauley, proprietor of the Mountain House inn atop Glacier Point, pushed the glowing remains of a campfire over the edge. Fueled by the rush of air as they fell, the coals splintered in orange sparks off the cliff face, a startling sight in the dark. The fall was an instant hit with visitors on the Valley floor, and McCauley, understanding the value of such an attraction to his mountaintop concession, began collecting fees to stage more firefalls.

The innkeeper put his twin sons, Frank and John, to work on the Firefall when they were eight years old. The father "bought each of us a jackass," which the boys rode down the Four Mile Trail to school every day, recalled Frank McCauley (as recounted in Hank Johnston's pictorial history, *The Yosemite Grant: 1864–1906*). "If a tourist wanted a Firefall, we collected $1.50, the standard fee, before we rode back up the trail to Glacier Point. We had a pack animal that we used to carry provisions for the hotel on our return trip. On the Fourth of July, a collection often amounted to ten or twenty dollars. Then my brother and I were packing wood out to the point on our jackasses for at least two days."

In 1897 McCauley quit his Mountain House concession, and the Firefall was temporarily discontinued. David Curry, who established the Curry Company tent-camping concession on the Valley floor in 1899, brought it back in relatively short order. He understood, like McCauley, that the event could be profitable. He coordinated crews on Glacier Point to prep for the display, with men gathering the bark of the red fir (which produced the best embers), lighting the bonfires, and letting them burn down to hot coals. When the spectators had paid up and darkness descended, Curry, nicknamed "The Stentor," would commence a call-and-response with the fire tenders on the point, and the cascade would be launched. In later years, after David Curry's death, the call-and-response was formalized:

"Hello, Glacier Point!"

"Hello, Camp Curry!"

"Is the fire ready?"

"The fire is ready!"

"Let the fire fall!"

"The fire falls!"

It was, by all accounts, spectacular. "High up at Glacier Point the living embers slowly begin to fall and continue until they become a blazing stream of red and gold swaying in the wind while sparks fly off like stars," wrote Mrs. H. J. Taylor in 1936. "The stream grows smaller and smaller until it becomes a mere thread of gold drawing the curtain of night, and darkness descends." Another writer would remember the hushed silences that would follow the Firefall and the music that accompanied it.

Firefall took a couple of brief hiatuses in its long run. The first, from 1913 to 1917, is attributed by one historian to a disagreement between David Curry and the US Department of the Interior, which oversaw park operations, over plans to expand Camp Curry. The second was during World War II, though apparently the park did permit the Curry Company to stage a "near record-sized firefall" for the troops in 1943.

Firefall was discontinued in 1968. The crowds that gathered to view the displays had thickened on the roadways and in the meadows, stopping traffic and trampling the grass and wildflowers. The National Park Service was also becoming more sensitive to ecological issues, and harvesting the bark of red firs to feed the flames went against a strengthening preserva-tionist ethos. The park also questioned whether an artificial display like Firefall had a place in a park dedicated to the appreciation of nature.

Still, even the final Firefall was given an affectionate eulogy in a park service press release quoted on a pair of websites: "The Firefall, a fancy of James McCauley's that caught on, and was popular for almost a hun-dred years, died Thursday, January 25, 1968, in a blazing farewell. It was a dandy Firefall, fat and long, and it ended with an exceptionally brilliant spurt, the embers lighting the cliff as they floated slowly downward."

Yosemite Wildlife

The Yosemite Valley itself has, in recent years, been a death trap to all wildlife unfortunate enough to enter it.
—Major H. C. Benson, acting superintendent of Yosemite National Park, 1906

When it comes to wildlife in Yosemite, it's all about the bears. The bears stop traffic. The bears terrify hikers on the trail. The bears dumpster-dive. The bears dismantle cars to get at the coolers within.

None of this behavior is natural other than, perhaps, the capacity to terrify unwitting hikers. The genome of a black bear does not include the innate ability to remove the windshield of a minivan to get at the Cheerios scattered inside by toddlers.

What is encoded is the need to survive, and bears have also evolved to be both opportunistic and quick learners. If mama bear discovers that SUVs parked in a campground are a likely source of nourishment, she will teach her cubs the same. The idea of a minivan is, of course, a modern construct. But the idea that the humans who would develop Yosemite would end up providing a food source for bears—and that this symbiosis would lead to conflict—follows on like water falling over a precipice.

Of course, this troubled interconnectedness is not solely about the bears. They are just big, furry, unignorable focal points. Yosemite harbors the usual complement of wildland fauna, from the ground squirrel to the peregrine falcon. Each of these creatures has, in the natural history of the park, either had to overcome, or succumb to, the changes and challenges imposed by its development.

Big Bear, Dead Bear

Let's start with the icon. The California grizzly bear is now extinct, but it holds a special place in the story of Yosemite National Park. One derivation of the park's name, Yosemite, could be from the Ahwahneechee *uzamati*, believed to mean "grizzly bear." The last band of Indians to inhabit the park were known to settlers as the "Grizzlies." The presence of the bear is integral to the Valley's native history, from the story of the raising of El Capitan to the belief that, because Yosemite was a "favorite resort" for the massive bears, the tribe that lived among them must be just as fierce. And, ominously, the first white men to look into the Indians' secret valley were a pair of prospectors hunting a grizzly.

The mythology of the bear extends far beyond Yosemite's boundaries. "Grizzly bear shamans," integral to the cultural histories of many California tribes, were considered both "outlaws and visionaries," endowed with supernatural powers employed for evil or for good. "It was believed that one way or another, these shamans could turn themselves into grizzlies, that they could travel great distances during the night and appear unexpectedly a hundred miles away. They were powerful people and almost invulnerable," writes historian Arthur Dawson.

The grizzly would become a symbol of power of the state as well. The "golden bear" graces California's state flag; in fact, the bruin was impressive enough to be chosen twice, both at the time of the Bear Flag Revolt, and later, when statehood had been formalized. The California grizzly is the mascot of the University of California, Berkeley. The school has close ties to Yosemite, from the cadre of Cal professors instrumental in founding the Sierra Club to research ongoing in the park today. Theodore Roosevelt, the president who would champion national parks and national forests, is commemorated by, among other things, the "teddy" bear.

Thousands of California grizzlies once roamed the mountains, meadows, and woodlands of the state. They were terrifying and aggressive, and as prospectors and others flooded into gold country—bear territory—in the mid-nineteenth century, hunting the animals proceeded unchecked. As one Yosemite ranger writes, killing a grizzly was, at the time, "the American equivalent of slaying a dragon in the wilds of the frontier."

It didn't take long to extirpate the massive bruins. The last California grizzly was killed in 1922 near Sequoia & Kings Canyon National Park; no wild grizzly has been seen in the state since 1924. The last Yosemite grizzly was killed in 1895, according to Yosemite's *Ranger Notes*. And the grizzly that reportedly was the model for the state flag? Called Monarch, he was captured in southern California in 1889 as part of a "publicity stunt" manufactured by newspaper magnate William Randolph Hearst, and kept in a San Francisco zoo until his death in 1911. His remains were donated to science, and his taxidermied pelt has been periodically displayed at the California Academy of Sciences in San Francisco.

The extinction of the California grizzly, *Ursus arctos californicus*, left California with a single bear species, the black bear, *Ursus americanus*. Differences in size and temperament help account for the black bears' endurance. Significantly, black bears are decidedly less confrontational than grizzlies, though if provoked, black bears have been known to gore and kill humans. But it's common knowledge that most black bears can be scared away from camps, trails, and homes by making loud noises— shouting, banging pots and pans, blowing a whistle. "Yell at the bear like you're the boss," advises a Yosemite ranger in a blog post, and it will "almost always" run off.

The black bear is also considerably smaller than the grizzly: While the largest black bear captured in Yosemite tipped the scale at nearly 700 pounds, Monarch weighed in at more than 1,100 pounds. Most black bears in Yosemite (and elsewhere) weigh between 150 and 250 pounds, depending on sex, age, and time of year.

Those differences don't mean black bear populations weren't impacted by hunting in California's frontier days. They were killed for their meat, to stop them raiding human foodstocks and livestock, and because people were afraid of them. Black bears aren't necessarily black, but can be very dark brown, cinnamon, even blonde, so relying on color alone to differentiate a black bear from a grizzly was not foolproof.

Unlike the grizzly, when faced with the human flood of the gold rush, enough black bears retreated into the wilderness for the species to survive. Most black bears occupy a historic range in the Sierra Nevada; they weren't commonly found in the Central Valley and coastal mountains because that was the grizzly's turf. Though their numbers diminished in those years, their habitual terrain offered protection, and they were able to rebound. In recent years, California's Department of Fish and Wildlife estimates that more than thirty thousand black bears reside in the state; black bears in Yosemite National Park number between three hundred and five hundred. They have, for better or worse, found refuge in places like Yosemite, Sequoia & Kings Canyon, protected wilderness and parkland around Lake Tahoe, and farther north in Lassen Volcanic National Park. Parklands like these, intended as preserves, would seem perfect habitat for these wild creatures. Unfortunately, it's not that simple.

Fed Bear, Dead Bear

Black bears are big eaters. In late summer and fall, when they are preparing to hibernate, the bears can consume an impressive 15,000 to 20,000 calories each day. When not hibernating or preparing to hibernate, they'll consume 5,000 to 8,000 calories a day.

Their traditional diet, unaugmented by humans, consists of acorns, grasses, berries, grubs and insects, fish, and mammals (if they could kill them or scavenge their carcasses). Yosemite after the arrival of American settlers offered additional culinary delights. Some could be called "natural," such as apples from the trees planted by homesteaders on the Valley floor. Others were accidental, like the contents of the proverbial picnic basket left unattended on a camp table, or food waste unearthed from one of the park's dump sites.

Things took a turn toward the deliberate, however, in the 1920s, when a series of poor decisions on the part of park administrators and concessionaires led to the intentional feeding of bears for fun and profit. The park essentially formalized a worrisome trend among Yosemite's black bears, which regularly dined on refuse in the park's dumps. The idea was twofold: First, by providing a formalized feeding area, hungry bears would be diverted away from campgrounds and cabins, where they posed a potential threat to safety. Second, the viewing public, already entranced by watching the "antics" of the bears while they fed, could be both satisfied

A radio operator has a close encounter with one of Yosemite's black bears.
PHOTO: JAMES V. LLOYD, CIRCA 1920. NATIONAL PARK SERVICE HISTORIC PHOTOGRAPH
COLLECTION.

and supervised. The dumps, called "bear pits," became essentially "bear shows."

An element of the bizarre crept into the equation as well, when one of the park's concessionaires, the Yosemite National Park Company, was permitted to pour crankcase oil over food in the dumps so that bears could be redirected to a lighted feeding platform the company had constructed. The concessionaire provided park visitors with transportation to the platform so they could observe the animals—for a fee, of course. The idea of wildlife on display was in keeping with another Yosemite attraction of the time: a zoo, established in 1918, in which mountain lions, deer, and a bear were kept in cages for visitors' amusement.

Shockingly, the close interaction between park visitors and black bears didn't result in radical numbers of deaths. The authors of *Off the Wall: Death in Yosemite* don't attribute a single death in the park to black bears, though they (and others) chronicle a harrowing number of close calls. In the 1920s and '30s, despite the formalized pits, incidents of park visitors being injured while feeding bears grew ever more frequent, with reported single-season encounters numbering in the forties, fifties, and sixties in those two decades.

Park administrators struggled to come up with a palatable solution as visitors and residents began to lose patience with bears looking for hand-outs. The practice of feeding bears in the park had habituated the animals, with unhealthy, unnatural consequences that would persist for decades. It wasn't just the bear pits; the park also maintained a fish hatchery between 1927 and 1956 near Happy Isles (as well as one near Wawona), and bears could feed there as well. Despite the pits and platforms, bears continued to scavenge and beg in the camps and at lodges. "Problem bears," responsible for repeated car break-ins and fearlessly foraging in tents and cabins, began to impact park visitation. Ironically, the park concessionaire, while still maintaining its feeding platform, would also lodge a complaint. The Curry Housekeeping Camp was forced to close early in 1927 "because of the fact that our guests simply would not endure the bear nuisance"; and park administrators were admonished to do something about the situation.

The fallback solution, unfortunately, was to kill the troublesome bears. But park service officials within Yosemite and at the national level, hoping to avoid the criticism that would follow, sought an answer that balanced two national park mandates: to promote visitation and to protect resources, including wildlife. Recognizing that what was happening was not the bears' fault, Carl P. Russell, then Yosemite's park naturalist (and later its superintendent), was among those who bucked against the idea of shooting the "victims." Rather than killing a mama bear with cubs that sent a number of people who had attempted to feed her to the park hospital, Russell proposed placing "responsibility upon the foolish visitors who insist on feeding her, and her cubs, from their hands. She injured no one who left her alone."

Though especially troublesome animals would continue to be destroyed, the park service initiated a relocation program, transporting problem bears from the Valley floor into the backcountry. The first bear traps were low-tech but functional, composed of logs or a section of corrugated metal pipe with a trapdoor and baited with a piece of meat. The problem? The bears came back. And why wouldn't they, when the Yosemite Valley was, and is, a cornucopia.

While the park discouraged hand-feeding bears early on, the bear pits endured into the 1960s. In 1963 the "Leopold Report," written by a team led by A. Starker Leopold, son of famed ecologist/writer Aldo Leopold, delineated how the National Park Service could ensure that its parks accomplish one of the primary motivations behind their creation, to "represent a vignette of primitive America." Among the recommendations: No bears should be fed in the parks. "Wildlife should not be displayed in fenced enclosures; this is the function of a zoo, not a national park. In the same category is artificial feeding of wildlife. Fed bears become bums, and dangerous," Leopold and his colleagues wrote. And Yosemite's bear pits were closed forever.

But problems persisted. As park visitation soared—more than two million people visited Yosemite each year in the late 1960s and early 1970s—so did the number of "damage incidents." The park service, feeling the heat, resorted to expedient means—it would admit to having destroyed more than two hundred "garbage bears" between 1960 and 1973. Noted photographer and mountaineer Galen Rowell wrote about the carnage in a 1974 edition of the *Sierra Club Bulletin*, including photographs of bear carcasses that had been dumped below one of the highways leading into the park. Rowell decried the "secrecy" with which the culling was carried out, the park's lack of a formal policy for dealing with nuisance bears, and the callousness of the manner in which the bear carcasses were disposed of. A public outcry ensued, with citizens writing to newspapers castigating the park for its actions. Others, however, supported the park, citing how out of control the bears in Yosemite had become.

With the media spotlight illuminating every move, the park instituted a formal bear management plan in 1975. The program had five objectives: to educate the public on how to properly store food in Yosemite; to remove artificial food sources; to enforce regulations prohibiting the feeding of wildlife; to remove problem bears; and to research and monitor the results.

Education was successful and is ongoing. In campgrounds, bear-proof trash receptacles were installed; the tricky handles stump the bears, but most humans can figure them out. In the backcountry, trekkers were required to carry bear-proof food canisters and educated on how to hang their food in bear bags so that the temptations within weren't easy pickings. To this day, schoolchildren attending environmental education programs are taught to properly dispose of every morsel of food, either by consuming it (eat that apple core!) or by wrapping it in a bandana and stashing it in a backpack to be thrown away properly upon return to camp.

Vehicle damage was, and still is, a problem. Bears associate cars with treats, and one study even determined that bears most often target minivans (with SUVs a close second) as potential food sources. While the study authors admit they can't prove why, they do acknowledge that vehicles carrying small children are worthy of additional study. Maybe the windows on minivans are easier to pop open? Maybe coolers are more visible when left in the back? And then there are the Cheerios wedged into seat cushions. While banning minivans has not been an option, the park has gone so far as to close campgrounds to discourage bears from learning that vehicles found there likely contain edibles. Bears have also been "hazed"—shot with rubber bullets, slingshots, and pepper spray—to discourage them from associating people and their vehicles with food.

The relocation element of the plan has proven trickier. Bears were relocated more than three hundred times between 1974 and 1977, some more than once, according to park literature. The animals essentially were given three strikes; on the third, particularly if they'd caused injury or property damage, they were destroyed. Unfortunately the implementation of the plan corresponded to a drought, which impacted natural food sources and resulted in the bears' seeking out camp foods. As one Yosemite ranger would blog, the joke was "that some bears beat the wildlife truck back to the Valley."

Ultimately, however, the management plan has been a positive for both bears and humans. In 2014, researchers with the University of California, Santa Cruz, reported that the amount of human food bears were consuming in Yosemite had returned to levels predating the troublesome 1920s: "The average figures for the proportion of human food in bear diets during the four time periods in the study were 13 percent for the period from 1915 to 1919; 27 percent for 1928 to 1939; 35 percent for 1975 to 1985; and 13 percent again for 2001 to 2007."

By 2015, bear incidents resulting in damage to property or vehicles (not necessarily injury), were down 94 percent since 1998, when more than 1,500 bear problems were reported. And it's not entirely an issue of "fed bear equals dead bear" anymore, as exemplified by the "red bear equals dead bear" signs now seen along park highways, advising drivers to slow down to avoid collisions with the bruins. Where once "bear jams," in the Yellowstone National Park viewing tradition, were an issue in Yosemite, now it's bear crashes that stop traffic. With luck, educating people will resolve this bear-human issue too.

Beyond the Bears

In Yosemite's pioneering days, few recognized the intimate interplay between the ecosystems of the park and the wild creatures that inhabited it. Hunting was a way of life, not only around the future park, but all across the American West. If settlers could kill it and eat it, they did. If they could kill it and make a dollar off its pelt, they did. If they could kill it to keep it from killing them, they did. Little thought was given to the fact that, by decimating the local herds of mule deer, hunters also threatened the animals that preyed on them with oblivion. For Yosemite's grizzly and for the Sierra Nevada bighorn sheep, hunting meant extinction.

Humans brought an additional scourge into Yosemite: domestic animals that transmitted disease to the park's endemic wildlife. Those Yosemite bighorns that survived arrows and bullets faced that additional threat, as sheepherders' flocks infected herds with contagions the native animals could not fend off. Domestic sheep were a pet peeve of John Muir's. Having worked a season as a sheepherder in the Sierra, he'd seen firsthand the damage the animals could do to mountain meadows and the habitat of the future park's native creatures. Later in the park's history, its deer population faced a similar infective threat: Foot-and-mouth disease carried by domestic livestock infected wild populations. As a result, the unhealthy animals were culled in great numbers.

In modern times, the application of pesticides on farmland miles away introduced poisons that worked up through the food chain and decimated raptor populations in Yosemite and throughout the United States.

And to this day, speeding tourists armed with automobiles take a toll on deer, bear, squirrels, rodents, and themselves.

Fortunately, the idea of wildlife conservation has, from the outset, been an integral component of Yosemite National Park's management, though it may have been misguided at times, or simply not put into practice. Even as the black bear was being habituated in the 1920s, the park's wildlife was blessed with a singular champion, San Francisco native George Melendez Wright. A graduate of the University of California, Berkeley, an explorer, a lover of nature, and an "ornithologist of note," Wright found employment as a naturalist in Yosemite, where he began cataloging such things as the impact of feeding black bears within the park and of unchecked hunting on the park's deer population. His pioneering studies would lead to scientific service on a national level; by the time he died—at age thirty-one, in a car accident while scouting potential park properties in New Mexico—Wright had become the first chief of the National Park Service's Wildlife Division, and was also head of the National Resources Board. Wright's approach to wildlife conservation, based on careful study and science, would become the foundation of ongoing wildlife conservation in the park and beyond.

But despite Wright's insights, and those of visionary conservationists like Muir, Galen Clark, and UC Berkeley's Joseph Grinnell, who conducted the groundbreaking Yosemite Transect Survey to document the park's animal life as completely as possible for future study, wildlife in Yosemite National Park does not lead a halcyon existence. The bears may have liked the freebies humans left for them in the bear pits, but ultimately, they paid a heavy toll. So too, in other ways and for other reasons, have the bears' wild compatriots.

BIG CATS

After the extirpation of the grizzly, the mountain lion became the primary predator in Yosemite. Cougars targeted livestock as well as their natural prey, the favorite being the mule deer. But humans were also potential quarry. While not a big threat in Yosemite, outside the park the big cats did, and still can, raise havoc. They are powerful, elusive, extremely efficient hunters.

A bounty was placed on California's mountain lions in 1915, and Yosemite's cougars were not immune. The state hired an official mountain lion hunter, Jay Bruce, who would kill more than six hundred pumas during his tenure, including a number of cats in the national park. Bruce was responsible for the deaths of forty-three mountain lions in Wawona and elsewhere in 1927 alone. In 1918, the hunter gave three cubs to the park after killing the mother in Wawona; only one female, bottle-raised, would survive. She became the Wawona lioness, star of the Yosemite zoo, a reportedly gentle creature that would keep her claws retracted when playing with children in her cage. "The animal was kitten-like in demeanor, romping with the children and chasing a ball in playful fashion," wrote Joseph Grinnell and Tracy Storer in *Animal Life in Yosemite*, published by the University of California's Museum of Vertebrate Zoology in 1924.

Mountain lions, like black bears, would eventually be redeemed. Their role in healthy ecosystems has since been studied and documented, in the spirit of Grinnell and Wright. In 1990, voters in the state passed Proposition 117, which bans mountain lion hunting in California. As of 2003, eighteen big cats (likely more) were thought to roam territories that encompassed sections of Yosemite National Park.

Deer

The fact is, visitors to Yosemite and elsewhere are more likely to be attacked by a deer than by any other large mammal in the park. That's true across the United States, in fact. The headline terrors—sharks, bears, big cats, vipers—all take their toll, but deer do the most damage. They startle and charge, using their antlers and hooves when they become aggressive, causing serious injury. In *Off the Wall: Death in Yosemite*, the authors recount the tragic story of a young boy who lost his life after being gored by a deer in the park. The upshot: Whether or not this boy had fed the deer himself, hand-feeding deer—or any wildlife—can produce disastrous results. Deer are meant to be wild, and when they are fed, they lose the natural caution that protects both animal and visitor.

Prior to the "discovery" of the Yosemite Valley in 1851, deer populations in what would become the national park were balanced by predation. They were hunted by people, mountain lions, and, to some extent, by bear, other wildcats, and coyotes. As settlers began to crowd the Valley and the high country, the range of the mule deer was cropped, much as the territory of the bear had been.

For deer, as for bear, the 1920s were pivotal. In this decade, the scourge of foot-and-mouth disease, which affects both livestock and hooved wild animals, spread through the Yosemite area (and other parts of California). A reported 22,000 deer were harvested in an effort to control the spread of the disease, which resulted in the near eradication of the animals from the Valley.

To help in the rebound, the park's deer were protected, and even coddled. Ranger Bill Reymann hand-fed the animals, an act that would, in modern times, be unlawful. But the tactic worked: The population grew. Unfortunately, some park visitors mimicked Ranger Reymann's tactics, which habituated the deer. By the middle of the twentieth century, the park was receiving complaints about begging deer, much like there were complaints about begging bears.

Education, as well as making the feeding of deer and other wildlife a crime, has tapered the incidents of conflict between deer and people in recent years. But deer, like other big game in Yosemite, still pose a hazard on roadways, where collisions cause damage, injuries, and deaths.

Sierra Nevada Bighorn Sheep

It didn't take long for the majestic bighorn sheep of Yosemite's high country to disappear from the landscape. By the 1870s, just twenty years after the gold rush, Joseph Grinnell and his team reportedly only found "stragglers" on their Yosemite Transect Survey. By 1890, when Yosemite National Park was established, not a single sheep could be found in the high country. They were gone.

Thousands of bighorn once ranged the rocky heights of the Sierra from north of Yosemite to south of Mount Whitney. They were John Muir's "animal mountaineers," gripping the granite with the soft, supple pads on their hooves, like the sticky rubber of a good climbing boot, and possessing the strength and balance to nimbly navigate the crags, cliffs, ledges, and talus that predominate above ten thousand feet.

In addition to their natural predators, including the puma, bighorns were hunted by the local tribes before the arrival of prospectors and homesteaders.

But the newcomers brought with them pressures that the herds could not withstand. Increased hunting took its toll, but disease was worse. Like the Indians, who had no immunity to pathogens imported by white settlers, the bighorn had no resistance to the blights carried by domestic sheep. Modern research, according to park literature, has shown that "nose-to-nose" contact between a wild sheep and a domestic sheep can initiate a "wildfire of death" that can flare through entire endemic populations. The onset of sheepherding in Yosemite in the late nineteenth century set such a blaze in motion.

The devastation wasn't limited to the park; it affected the bighorn across its range. By the time the sheep received protection from the state of California in 1882, only two herds remained. A paltry 125 bighorn were thought to be still living on the high ground.

Thirty-eight descendants of those survivors were relocated into Yosemite's high country in the 1980s, with the hope of repopulating the species' former turf around Tioga Pass. The effort—a collaboration between a number of federal and state agencies—started well, with the original number blossoming to one hundred. But for unknown reasons, the animals began dying again, and the herd size dropped dramatically in the early 1990s. The bighorns' survival is still a dance along a knife-edge, and it seems the sheep can lose their grip after all.

As of 2015, another rebound was under way, with an estimated six hundred sheep roaming the high country statewide, and forty or so living in or near Yosemite National Park. Protected with endangered status under the federal Endangered Species Act, the park hopes and expects that, with careful husbandry, bighorn sheep can reestablish stable populations throughout its former range.

Peregrine Falcons

The park's peregrine falcons have done what wildlife experts hope the bighorn sheep can do—staged a turnaround and reclaimed their historic homes on Yosemite's magnificent cliffs.

The raptors didn't fall victim to prospectors or settlers in the early days of the park. Their downfall was born in the mid-twentieth century, when chemical pesticides and herbicides began to be applied with abandon in California's Central Valley, by this time a national breadbasket.

The culprit was dichlorodiphenyltrichloroethane, more commonly called DDT, which was used in the latter part of World War II to destroy pests that caused disease among the troops. Rachel Carson's seminal book, *Silent Spring*, published in 1962, unveiled the havoc wreaked by the unchecked and unstudied spraying of DDT and other chemicals on the food supply, arguing that these compounds caused disease and death all the way up the food chain, from the insects at the bottom, which they were intended to kill, to the humans and predators at the top, including raptors.

For the birds, concentrations of DDT caused the shells of their eggs to thin, so that nesting pairs would crush their offspring just trying to warm or protect them. Raptor populations in Yosemite and elsewhere plummeted, and the peregrine, like the bighorn, was federally designated an endangered species.

When DDT was identified as the source of the widespread decline in peregrines and other raptors—and after contentious lawsuits and hearings, which helped to lay the foundation for the modern environmental movement—use of the insecticide was banned. Again, with careful husbandry and through relocation programs, the peregrine was reestablished in the park. In fact, the peregrine's recovery has been so successful across its range that it has been delisted as an endangered species.

The story of the peregrine reverberates. To this day, the distrust spawned in the battle over DDT informs wildlife policy decisions and feeds modern arguments about how human interference on a micro level—chemical pesticides, herbicides, food additives such as hormones and preservatives, genetically modified organisms—can affect the macro.

SHARING THE SPACE

Learning how to live with wildlife, rather than removing it, is an ongoing process in Yosemite. In a park that has seen visitation mushroom into the millions, conflicts were essentially preordained. Profoundly, where once the blame and punishment for those conflicts fell on wildlife, now responsibility rests on the visitor. Conscientious behavior has not always been the primary concern of vacationers, but for lovers of wild places, from John Muir and Galen Clark onward, it has gained power over the

A coyote makes its way down the edge of Cook's Meadow. PHOTO: PENN CHOURRÉ

years. At an elemental level, the delicate balance needed to maintain a peaceful interface between wild creature and human has been restored. It's about the health and well-being of all involved—the bear, the deer, the sheep, the bird, and even the human behind the wheel of the innocent minivan.

Yosemite's Furies:
Wildfire, Rockfall, and Flood

Yosemite National Park is a wilderness wonderland. It's all good: Happy vacationers snap photos of world-famous sights; well-mannered wildlife is viewed from safe distances; picnics unfold in sun-dappled campgrounds; youngsters dip their feet in the placid waters of the Merced after a pleasant hike through whispering woodlands or along the edge of a towering cliff.

Well, most of the time, that is.

Wilderness is the operative word. At times, Yosemite simply can't behave like a wonderland. The very nature of its construction predicates rockfall, which can bury the campsite where the family has spent two weeks every summer in fresh talus. Well-meaning fire-suppression efforts have primed the woodlands for wildfire, which can transform a once-peaceful walk among the pines into an enervating trek through a scorched and creaking ghost forest. And these are mountains, so blizzards, rain-storms, and windstorms can be epic, unleashing floodwaters that can erase the riverside beaches where children once learned to fish.

But as far as wilderness is concerned, fire, flood, and rockfall are regenerative and transformative events. In Yosemite, where the tradition of research is as old as the park itself, careful study of the aftermath of these events is integral to understanding how best to conserve habitat and human and natural resources. Uncovering the progression of recovery from past events informs how the park responds to events that will occur in the future. These forces not only remodel the landscape, they also reshape Yosemite's culture.

WILDFIRE

The Rim Fire, which exploded in the Stanislaus National Forest in August 2013 and burned portions of Yosemite National Park's backcountry, is history made recently.

The scars left by the massive burn, which encompassed more than four hundred square miles, are still raw. Drive into the park along CA 120, the Big Oak Flat Road, and the scenery is desolate. The folded walls of the Tuolumne River canyon, up and down, water to sky, are stripped of forest; the exposed soil remains gray-red, with only a faint green blush of new growth visible more than two years after the blaze. The standing dead—trees with needles and branches torched off—line the ridgetops like totem poles. Some of the snags on slopes flanking the highway have been cut and hauled away so they can't become fuel for another fire. Others have been left upright, to provide habitat for birds and bats. And some remain where they fell, also providing habitat and feeding nutrients the baked soil as they rot away.

Dubbed a "mega-fire," the stats of the Rim Fire are staggering. As of early 2016, it remains the largest wildfire in the recorded history of California's Sierra Nevada. The plume reached four miles into the atmosphere, and its smoke fouled the air as far north as Reno and Lake Tahoe. It took 3,700 firefighters, using 460 fire trucks, 60 bulldozers, and 15 helicopters, more than nine weeks to contain. More than 110 structures were destroyed, and another 5,500 or so were threatened. The blaze also endangered San Francisco's water supply, impounded in the Hetch Hetchy Reservoir, and forced the closure of the Hetch Hetchy powerhouses, which provide electricity for the city's airport, hospitals, and other infrastructure. With tourism shut down by smoke and fear, local economies lost an estimated $1.8 billion. Millions of dollars were spent to fight the fire, an estimated $127 million on suppression alone. The economic and visual impacts are ongoing, with more than 33,000 acres of forest designated for salvage of standing and fallen trees in 2015.

The Rim Fire is the most recent, and most violent, of many fires to scorch Yosemite National Park. But before contact, conflagrations of this intensity were relatively unknown. That's not to say that forests in the Sierra Nevada and elsewhere in the West didn't burn; they did so regularly, with blazes occurring at intervals of between five and sixteen years. That regularity reduced the intensity of the fires, as fuels such as deadfall and duff couldn't accumulate. The growth rings of ancient sequoias on the west slope of the Sierra document fire scars going back three thousand years, and confirm the occurrence of regular understory-cleansing burns.

California Indians understood the importance of fire to the environment and the husbandry of their food sources. In the Yosemite Valley, charcoal dating back about nine thousand years has been found, indicating that the prehistoric people of *Ahwahnee* were lighting ground fires to clear the Valley floor so that black oaks, which provide acorns, wouldn't be crowded out by evergreens. Fire also rejuvenated seed-bearing grasses and fruiting plants. The practice was well established in the years before the Mariposa Battalion arrived, with the Ahwahneechee burning Yosemite's meadows every year before they descended to warmer elevations for the winter.

Once the Yosemite Indians were driven from their homeland, the regular ground fires ceased. Nearly eighty years after the "discovery" of Yosemite by the battalion, the last Ahwahneechee, Maria Lebrado, returned to the Valley. She saw the change—the damage—clearly, telling her companion, Mrs. H. J. Taylor, that the floor of *Ahwahnee*, once a "deep grassy valley," was "too dirty, too much brushy." The open fields where her people had once played ball games, and where the black oaks were nurtured, were now littered with the nuisance trees that fires had once kept at bay.

Yosemite Valley's next residents—ranchers and farmers—occasionally used ground fires to improve pasture, and their grazing livestock helped keep the fuel loads under control. If wildfire did ignite on the Valley floor, it generally burned uncontrolled from wall to wall or wall to river—again, clearing the fuels. Lumberjacks, on the other hand, suppressed fire to preserve stands of timber. In the woodlands, litter began to accumulate unchecked, setting the stage for conflagrations capable of burning hot, fast, and ferociously. When the Yosemite Grant was enacted in 1864, and later the national park established, the accumulations continued, with park superintendents focused on preserving the forests in every way, from uprooting commercial timber operations on inholdings to stamping out blazes wherever they flared up.

The practice of suppressing fires in Yosemite and throughout America's national parks and national forests was entrenched by the early 1900s. The US Forest Service—established in 1905, and headed by a thoughtful and politically powerful forester named Gifford Pinchot—was charged with the conservation of vast tracts of timberland throughout the West. Conservation, in Pinchot's view, meant putting those forests to their best use, which essentially translated to providing lumber for industry. A burned forest was worthless, so any blaze was extinguished as quickly as humanly possible.

That philosophy was bolstered in 1910, when lightning-caused wildfires in Montana, Idaho, and Washington State were whipped by hurricane-force winds into the Big Blowup, or the Big Burn. This infamous fire was so intense and moved so fast that, despite the extraordinary efforts of forest rangers turned fire captains, and a firefighting army composed of local residents, hired immigrants, and thousands of soldiers, the Big Burn consumed three million acres of wildland, destroyed several mountain towns, and killed a hundred people. In the aftermath, fire suppression became a forest management mandate. No fire was a good fire.

As the decades passed, deadfall, undergrowth, and dense mats of duff built up. The forests themselves thickened, became overcrowded, and drained nourishment from the soil, leading to disease and insect infestations. But suppressing fires, no matter their ability to clear out the worrisome accumulations of tinder, remained the primary focus of wildland managers. Yosemite was no exception: The park's 1964 Forest Fire Control Plan includes a quote from superintendent John Preston that expresses the prevailing view. "Fire suppression takes precedence over all other park activities except the saving or safeguarding of human life."

By the 1980s, however, science began to give foresters deeper insight into the role regular wildfires played in the health of the forests, and also enlightened them as to the unfortunate consequences of the aggressive suppression regime. Wildfires now burned faster and hotter, consuming fuels that should have burned off years before. To rectify the situation, in the 1990s, the forest service, the national parks, and the Bureau of Land Management embraced plans that allow some wildfires to burn themselves out. They also began setting prescribed or controlled burns, with the hope of clearing accumulated fuels so that a fire, if it did begin, might not be as destructive. In the late twentieth century, and into the early 2000s, more than two hundred prescribed burns, most less than one thousand acres in size, were set to clear the hazards in and around Yosemite National Park.

But despite planning and preparation, some wildfires were massively destructive. On August 7, 1990, lightning ignited a blaze called the Arch Rock, or A-Rock, Fire, on the north side of the Merced River canyon at the western boundary of the park. Another fire, the Steamboat, flared up on the south side of the Merced River gorge. These two blazes burned for a week before they were mostly contained, creating a plume of smoke that rose 30,000 feet high. A firestorm from the A-Rock whipped through tiny Foresta, destroying more than sixty cabins, turning propane tanks into bombs, and melting vehicles. Other structures were torched in El Portal, and the Steamboat Fire threatened Yosemite West. More than 15,000 people were evacuated from the park, which was closed for a week. In the end, despite the efforts of more than 3,000 firefighters, A-Rock burned more than 17,000 acres, and Steamboat, more than 6,000.

In 1996 the Ackerson Fire, the largest in Yosemite's recorded history, blew through about 47,000 acres in the northwest portion of the park, near Hetch Hetchy. Other significant fires or fire complexes have followed on—the Cottonwood, Harden, Big Meadow, and Grouse fires flared up in 2009; the Rim Fire in 2013; the Meadow, El Portal, and Dog Rock fires in 2014; the Tenaya Fire in 2015. Drought conditions and fuels built up in the era of suppression have primed the park and surrounding forests for hot, hard burns into the foreseeable future.

Which is not to say that rangers with the park service and the forest service have thrown up their hands. It happens every year: Rangers and firefighters head off into the woods with chain saws and hand tools to gather downed wood and stack it in piles or pyramids. Then they wait for the first rains or snows, which make it safe to ignite prescribed burns. Like the Indians, they're using fire to cleanse the forest, keep it healthy, and, hopefully, reduce the risk of a wildfire becoming an inferno.

In the wake of a blaze like A-Rock or the Rim, it's tough to see any redemptive value in fire. But it's there. Communities come together to offer support and consolation, and to help rebuild. Firefighters and land managers gain insight into the vagaries of wildfire behavior, which may help keep lives and property safe in the next blowup. And it's heartening to know that, even in the heat of battle, firefighters do what they do with grace and humor. On the cover of one of the daily bulletins (called "Hot Flashes") from the 1990 fires, a cartoon shows one ranger telling another: "You realize that if they had called that fire across the Merced [the Steamboat] 'a hard place,' we'd be stuck between A-Rock and A Hard Place!"

The resilience of the natural world reveals itself more slowly, year by year, but persistently. Venture into a burn zone in the spring following the fire, and the first signs are there. Woodpeckers drum in the treetops, a steady beat amid the creaking and groaning of the dead standing. Hints of green, perhaps shoots of purple bloom, edge the ash piles and the blackened craters of fallen trees. Walk in the burn zone fifteen years later, and sad, negative words do not apply. Visitors entering the park along the

The smoke plume from 2015's Tenaya Fire billows over the Yosemite Valley Rim.
COURTESY OF THE NATIONAL PARK SERVICE

Big Oak Flat Road in the years immediately following the Rim Fire may bemoan how "ugly" the fire scars are, but ecologists and biologists watch the recovery with amazement and joy. It may take decades, but even soils sterilized by the intense heat of the historic blaze will someday support a mighty, lovely, healthy woodland.

ROCKFALL

On the evening of July 10, 1996, a massive granite arch detached from the cliff face between Glacier Point and Washburn Point, high above Happy Isles. Split in two pieces, the arch slid about 800 feet down a steep sloping apron, then launched into a free fall. When the slabs hit the Valley floor, about 1,800 feet below, they detonated, creating a blast of wind that traveled outward at nearly 200 miles per hour. The surrounding forest— mature evergreens of substantial girth—was blown flat for a half-mile. A man was killed by one of those falling trees, and several other people were injured. But, given the size of the rockfall, the time of year, and the fact that campgrounds, trailheads, a shuttle stop, and a nature center are at the base of the wall, it's a miracle more people weren't lost.

The Happy Isles rockfall was a colossal reminder that, while Yosemite's granite walls are fiercely beautiful and ostensibly concrete, they flex and stretch, and pieces regularly peel off. No cliff is immune. That ability to fail—often on a mammoth scale—is baked into the rock. The cliffs are the exposed faces of a huge batholith formed under great heat and pressure many thousands of years ago, thrust upward and chiseled by glaciers, a masterwork of plate tectonics and ice. That ancient pressure—or rather, the release of that pressure—creates cracks in the granite. Then time and erosion go to work: trickling water; freeze and thaw; the creeping root systems of trees and plants, singly or in concert, nudging and weakening the granite where it has fractured. When the force of gravity exceeds the elemental glue—well, it's all downhill from there.

The stats of the Happy Isles rockfall are as impressive as those of the Rim Fire in their own way. Geologists estimate that the arch weighed about 90,000 tons and was "about 18 feet thick and the size of a football field," according to Allen Glazner and Greg Stock, authors of *Geology Underfoot in Yosemite National Park*. When the twin slabs, unleashed fourteen seconds apart, hit the ground, they were likely traveling in excess of 260 miles per hour. The impact tripped seismographs, used to measure earthquakes, more than 100 miles away, registering a magnitude of 2.15, and representing "the largest vertical rock free-fall ever recorded seismically." About one thousand trees were leveled in the windblast, some uprooted, others snapped. Boulders destroyed a bridge and snack bar, but miraculously left the Happy Isles Nature Center intact. The explosion of the blocks generated a cloud of pulverized granite and dust that ballooned two thousand feet upward and ricocheted off the opposite wall, then lingered, hampering search-and-rescue operations as night fell.

A US Geological Survey report on the event records the observations of Ernie Milan, who was working on the John Muir Trail when the rockfall occurred. "[H]e heard a roaring sound, like a jet engine, close overhead, then saw a dark billowy cloud moving slowly and quietly from the impact area on the talus toward the Happy Isles Nature Center. [H]e noted that the sky went black for six minutes as the dust raised by the cloud blocked out the late afternoon light." Likened to a volcanic pyroclastic flow, the "cauliflower-like" bloom of rock and dust flowed across the flats and then rebounded off Grizzly Peak before it began to settle.

The Happy Isles rockfall is remarkable because the blocks of granite made it to the Valley floor intact, which accounts for the bomb-like destructive force. But Happy Isles, while novel, is not Yosemite's biggest rockfall, or its first—and it certainly won't be the last. On average at least one slope fails every week somewhere in the park; more rockslides occur in Yosemite than in any other national park. At least one thousand major rockfalls have been recorded since the late 1850s, when settlers began to keep written records. Of those documented events, park records list the 1987 Middle Brother rockfall as among the largest. Because the exfoliated granite broke up as it slid down the mountainside, as happens in most rockfalls, the size of the slide is measured in volume—785,000 cubic yards, or 1.8 million tons. Glazner and Stock put this in terms a bit more comprehensible: The debris could fill about 65,000 dump trucks. As with Happy Isles, the collapse created a thick dust cloud, and the rubble closed Northside Road, but no one was injured in the slide.

Though not nearly as large, the most eloquently described Yosemite rockfall occurred following a large earthquake on the east side of the Sierra Nevada in 1872. John Muir was a resident of the Valley at the time, and would, of course, write about it. As the earth began to shake, Muir dashed out of his cabin, "both glad and frightened, shouting, 'A noble earthquake!' feeling sure I was going to learn something."

The young naturalist found his footing as the initial shock subsided, then began scanning the walls for evidence that such temblors were responsible for the talus fields he'd observed around the Valley floor. He didn't have to wait long: "It was a calm moonlight night, and no sound was heard for the first minute or two save a low muffled underground rumbling and a slight rustling of the agitated trees, as if, in wrestling with the mountains, Nature were holding her breath. Then, suddenly, out of the strange silence and strange motion there came a tremendous roar. The Eagle Rock, a short distance up the valley, had given way, and I saw it falling in thousands of the great boulders I had been studying so long, pouring to the valley floor in a free curve luminous from friction, making a terribly sublime and beautiful spectacle."

The young Muir then did with enthusiasm that which most sane people would never contemplate: He climbed onto the still-settling rubble, observing the dust that puffed from between the rocks and breathing in "the odor of crushed Douglas Spruces, from a grove that had been mowed down and mashed like weeds."

In that same quake another huge block, estimated to have weighed more than 100,000 tons, fell from Liberty Cap, and geologists believe it created an air blast like the one that toppled the trees at Happy Isles more than one hundred years later. The evidence: La Casa Nevada, the hotel that Albert and Emily Snow operated on the plateau between Vernal and Nevada Falls, "moved two inches to the east," according to an account written by Yosemite guardian Galen Clark.

Geologists also found the remains of an even larger rockfall near the Liberty Cap slide, a so-called "rock avalanche" that took place about 15,000 years ago, long before written records were kept. Yet another prehistoric rock avalanche deposited so much rock near the mouth of Tenaya Canyon—Stock and Glazner estimate the debris had the cubic yardage of a "good-sized suburb"—that it dammed the creek and created a large lake. Mirror Lake is the slowly disappearing remnant.

And it figures that one of the biggest rock avalanches in Yosemite Valley would lie at the base of the biggest monolith: El Capitan. That collapse comprised nearly four million cubic yards of material, sprawling more than four-tenths of a mile from the cliff base across the Valley floor. That event, which Stock believes happened about 3,600 years ago, may have corresponded to an earthquake along the same fault that shook the Valley in 1872.

Big or small, rockfall has taken a significant toll on life and property in the Valley. By one count, fifteen deaths and about seventy injuries can be attributed to rockfall in or near the park. Hikers, like the one killed by the falling tree in Happy Isles, are among the most likely to be caught in the wrong place at the wrong time. Among the first was Florence Hutchings, daughter of Yosemite pioneer James Hutchings, and the first white baby born in Yosemite. She was hiking in LeConte Gully when she was struck and killed by a falling boulder. She was seventeen.

And three hikers were killed in November 1980, when a slab broke away from the cliff above the Yosemite Falls Trail after the first freeze of the season. According to a park bulletin, before the slide, "sounds like gunfire were heard, as the slab began to give way, popping its last connections." The rock, weighing about 4,500 tons, shattered as it fell, taking out more than forty-three of the historic trail's famous switchbacks. In addition to the three deaths, a number of companion hikers were injured.

Climbers regularly get pinged by rockfall as well. Even with helmets, a single rock hurtling a thousand feet from above can injure or kill a person. If a flake pulls free of the cliff as a climber puts her weight on it, a fall is inevitable. Climbers listen, tap, inspect, and rig anchors on the cliffs they ascend, trying to protect against the threat of flaking rock. And climbing routes take a beating as well; a long section of one of the most iconic routes on Half Dome, the Regular Northwest Face, first ascended by a team that included Royal Robbins, peeled away in 2015, leaving a pale scar on the lichen-stained wall.

As far as infrastructure is concerned, Curry Village, at the base of Glacier Point, has taken its share of hits. When the tent camp rings with the clatter of smaller rocks skittering down the cliffs that loom above, visitors instinctively look up and back away. Many recall a pair of rockfalls in October 2008 that took out seventeen cabins in the village and forced the permanent closure of nearly three hundred tents and employee housing units.

El Portal Road (CA 140) has also taken a beating. In the spring of 1982 a portion of the Cookie Cliff, near the Arch Rock entrance, collapsed onto the roadway, depositing huge boulders that had to be blasted clear. Elephant Rock, on the opposite side of the Merced River Gorge, is also subject to rockfall; geologists note events along this stretch have pinched the Merced in a "rockslide dam." Farther downstream, travelers must detour around the 2006 Ferguson rockslide, which buried the roadway under more than twenty-one million cubic feet of rock.

One of Yosemite's biggest recent rockfall events occurred in 2009, when more than one hundred thousand tons of rock split off Ahwiyah

Rockfall obliterated a portion of the trail around Mirror Lake in 2009.
COURTESY OF THE NATIONAL PARK SERVICE

Point below Half Dome and cascaded into Tenaya Canyon, taking out a significant stretch of the trail around Mirror Lake. But it doesn't take that much rock to close a trail. In 2014, about sixteen tons of rock cascaded five hundred feet down a cliff face east of Wapama Falls in Hetch Hetchy, crushing trees and creating fresh boulders as it tumbled into the reservoir. About four hundred feet of the trail to Rancheria Falls was buried.

Unlike wildfire, there's really nothing park managers can do to mitigate rockfall. The various causes—rainfall, earthquakes, freeze–thaw, the infiltration of root systems—are all known, but what faces will give, and when, remains unpredictable. The signs are everywhere; rangers are watchful; geologists continue to study and hypothesize. The only sure thing is that the cliffs will continue to exfoliate, leaving bright white scars on gray granite and new boulders atop the old at the bottoms of the broken cliffs.

Flood

For the most part, central California's weather is enviably mild. Moderate temperatures and crystal-blue skies predominate in spring and fall; summers are hot and dry; cold, rain, and snow are mostly confined to a brief winter season. Cabin fever is not an issue anywhere in the state, as the weather breaks long before sanity does.

In a "normal" year, the first major winter storm hits the state in late October or early November, and snow falls in the Sierra Nevada with some regularity through March. Yosemite's high country will chill out under a thickening quilt of snow from December to April. While the depth of that blanket varies, several feet linger regardless of warm spells, deep enough for backcountry skiers and snowshoers to enjoy. In the Valley, given its low elevation, snow is less likely to stick. But it still falls, and when it's too warm for snow, it rains.

But in terms of moisture, California winters are notoriously fickle. The state ping-pongs between drought and what's become known, in modern times, as El Niño, a Pacific weather pattern that pumps moisture into storms that can march back-to-back across the state for weeks. In drought years, the high country may see so little snow that hiking trails are clear in March. In El Niño years, so much snow can fall that it may never completely melt off the north faces in summer.

The winter of 1996–1997 was an El Niño year.

Snow began accumulating early that winter, piling up in the high country so quickly that by late December the snowpack was estimated at 180 percent of normal. On New Year's Day 1997, what is known colloquially as a "Pineapple Express," a warm, moisture-laden storm originating over the Pacific, moved into the state. If it had been cooler, the storm would have added significantly to the snowpack. But it rained instead. Tioga Pass, at nearly ten thousand feet, saw rain. Four inches were dumped on the snow-burdened Tuolumne Meadows. The rain melted the snow, and the combined meltwater and rainfall poured off the saturated terrain, filling creeks that funnel down through the canyons and over Yosemite's cliffs into the Merced.

The river swelled to historic proportions, taking on the contours of a lake but with a vicious current, in what would become a record-setting flood. Glazner and Stock provide yet another masterful visual for understanding the Merced's peak flow, which measured 24,000 cubic feet per second at Pohono Bridge. "A cubic foot of water weighs about 63 pounds, so that means about 1.55 million pounds of water was flowing past the bridge *each second*," the geologists explain in *Geology Underfoot*. "This is the equivalent of about 337 Ford Explorers—each second."

Another way to quantify the magnitude of the New Year's Flood is to compare the flows to normal. Typically, the volume of the Merced in the runoff season is about five thousand cubic feet per second. By fall, after a long, dry summer, the river flows at about fifteen cubic feet per second. And it's impressive even then.

And yet another measure: Take a walk through the meadows and across the bridges on the Valley floor, where signs have been erected marking high water. You'll be looking up at them. There's no way, on a quiet autumn day, standing on the Sentinel Bridge, gazing up at the sign with the river rolling placidly below, to visualize the velocity. But the depth is aptly illustrated.

Video of the event shows a roiling Merced, tossing logs against bridges and spinning around trees and signs, chewing off chunks of asphalt roadway. The muddy water sprawls across the meadows, raindrops pelting the surface. The major falls shoot off the cliffs like water cannons, flying clear of the faces in massive white flumes.

About two thousand people were stranded in the Valley by the floodwaters, but no one was injured. Much of the infrastructure in low-lying areas on the Valley floor, however, was demolished. The riverside campgrounds, especially in the east end of the Valley, were completely inundated; about four hundred campsites were permanently destroyed. Buildings in the Housekeeping Camp and at Yosemite Lodge were damaged, along with administrative structures on both sides of the river, but the Ahwahnee Hotel, Curry Village, and other structures on higher ground were largely spared. The meadows were submerged, their trails obliterated. Bridges were damaged. Downstream, an eight-mile stretch of the El Portal Road was consumed, and hotels and park structures in El Portal were flooded. The cost to repair: more than $175 million. The park was closed for more than two months to repair, rebuild, and recover.

The rain-on-snow scenario that spawned the 1997 New Year's Flood can set the stage for avalanche as well as abrupt melting. John Muir witnessed such an event during his time in Yosemite, when a sudden, warm storm brought upon the Valley "a glorious flood." As the rain released high-country snow from winter's icy hold, it "rushed simultaneously from a thousand slopes in the wildest extravagance, heaving and swelling flood over flood, and plunging into the Valley in stupendous avalanches." The warm storm created waterfalls all around, Muir wrote. "I caught glimpses of more falls than I could readily count; while the whole Valley throbbed and trembled, and was filled with an awful, massive, solemn, sea-like roar."

The park has experienced five "great" floods in its history, in 1937, 1950, 1955, 1964, and, obviously, 1997. Records from gauging stations at Happy Isles and the Pohono Bridge go back to 1916, but memorable floods predating those years, particularly in 1867 and 1890, are mentioned in park literature. Whether record-breaking or not, the floods etch themselves in memory and in story. The flood of December 1937 is remembered in one administrative history as a "disaster of unparalleled proportions; the formation of an immense lake [in Yosemite Valley] resulted in damage to road surfaces, businesses, and residences, and inundation of campgrounds." One ranger recalled the Merced overflowing its

The scar left by rockfall at Ahwiyah Point in 2009. COURTESY OF THE NATIONAL PARK SERVICE

banks in July 1995, forcing the evacuation of the park's campgrounds, with motor homes parked in the cleared areas around the visitor center and administrative buildings.

But of all the potential disasters that have, and can, alter Yosemite's physical and cultural status quo, flood is the most predictable. When El Niño is forecast, preparations can begin. People can evacuate or move to higher ground. Buildings can be sandbagged and equipment relocated. There's no moving a campground, or a roadway, or a trail, but after the flood, building on what's been learned, these can be redesigned or reconfigured in such a way that the next deluge might not be so damaging.

RESILIENCE

Wilderness ranger Mark Fincher called the 1990s Yosemite's "decade of disaster." The A-Rock and Steamboat Fires, the New Year's Flood, the Happy Isles rockfall, even a murder spree that claimed the lives of three park visitors and a park employee—these events are still vivid in the memories of those who endured them. But the park's guardians, informed by science and history, aren't defeated by the knowledge that another massive flood or fire is preordained. Instead, they study the woods and walls and weather with the goal of predicting the next "big thing," and prepare as best they can to protect lives and the landscape.

What's clear and sometimes overlooked is that each of these forces of nature has a cleansing effect. Even drought, which may be the next disaster the park faces, will clear detritus, eliminate the unfit, pave the way for the revival of a plant or creature that may have lain dormant for decades. Fire opens the cones and releases the seeds of the giant sequoia, and allows other "fire followers," like the pansy monkeyflower, to find a place in the sun. Floods open river channels and refresh riparian zones along the banks. Rockfalls rearrange topography and create habitat. Even the destruction of campsites, bridges, trails, and buildings has an upside: They can be improved, relocated, or simply not rebuilt at all. A Yosemite Valley minus four hundred campsites is a less-crowded Yosemite, a Yosemite closer, perhaps, to its ideal.

No matter how domesticated it appears, Yosemite is anchored in wildness. It's a park with attractions driven by elemental forces; Disneyland, for all its creativity, can't even begin to compete. Stories of fire and rockfall and flood may seem an extravagant way to make the point, but Yosemite's unpredictability is part of the magic of the place. It provides an edge that renders a wonderland in even sharper relief.

Appendix

Yosemite National Park Statistics

These numbers, pulled from the park website, define Yosemite as of 2014–2015. Some will be history shortly.

FAST FACTS

Annual visitation: ~4.1 million
Annual operating budget: $29 million
Number of National Park Service employees: 1,200 in summer, 800 in winter

Land encompassed within park boundaries: 1,169 square miles
Designated wilderness: ~704 million acres. Yosemite is 94 percent back-country. The "front country" is contained within the developed areas of the park: Yosemite Valley, Glacier Point and the Badger Pass Ski Area, Wawona, Foresta, Crane Flat, and the like.

Miles of paved roadway: ~214
Miles of graded roadway: ~68
Miles of trail: ~840
Miles of paved trail: ~20

Number of campsites available: ~1,530, including group camps
Number of lodging units available: ~1,400
Number of park service buildings: 747
Number of concession buildings: 386

Average annual snowfall in the high country: ~100 inches
Average annual snowfall in Yosemite Valley: ~30 inches

USAGE TRENDS

(from visitor surveys conducted in 2008–2009)

In winter:
- 90 percent were from California
- 25 percent were first-time visitors
- 85 percent self-identified as sightseers
- 35 percent self-identified as hikers

In summer:
- 60 percent were from California
- 25 percent were international visitors
- 60 percent were first-time visitors
- 93 percent self-identified as sightseers

WILDLIFE

- 90 mammal species
- 150 regularly occurring bird species
- 12 amphibian species
- 22 reptilian species

FLORA

- 1,500 species of flowering plants
- 30 tree species
- 36,000 acres of meadowland

ACKNOWLEDGMENTS

Researching this book was a bit like distilling the grapes of a thousand vineyards into a single bottle. Historical books, photos, and documents overflow the library in the attic of the Yosemite Museum into other libraries and annexes, from Berkeley's Bancroft to the Sierra Club's vaults. It was daunting, but with the guidance of colleagues, editors, and Yosemite's interpretive staff, I was able to make my way.

I am not the first to write about historic Yosemite. An army of writers and researchers have already pored over the original and secondary documents, and produced a rich and colorful trove of resources. Without their work these essays would have been impossible. I am most deeply indebted to Carl P. Russell, Shirley Sargent, Hank Johnston, Bill Roney, Albert Runte, Michael Ghigliere, Charles "Butch" Farabee Jr., and Linda W. Greene. The books they wrote were essential guides to Yosemite's vast historic reservoir. What's presented in these essays pulls from both first-hand and secondary sources. I am solely responsible for any mistakes of fact or interpretation they contain.

I am also forever grateful to Virginia Sanchez, Yosemite's research librarian, whose sage and witty advice helped to keep me focused. She was an invaluable resource in terms of sussing out what would be most useful to my endeavor during my too-brief visits to the Yosemite Research Library.

Access to original documents and research posted on the Internet was a lifesaver. The Yosemite National Park website, and other National Park Service websites, are vast and deep, rabbit holes of information that I plumbed repeatedly. So, too, the resources digitized at Yosemite Online by Dan Anderson. If I couldn't lay my hands on a hard copy of an original historical document or book, I often would find an electronic copy on this meticulously curated site.

Yosemite National Park's interpretive rangers provided a wealth of information in both formal presentations and informal discussions.

Thanks to Dean Shenk, Phil Johnson, Shelton Johnson, Julia Parker, Mark Fincher, Christine Loberg, Erik Westerlund, and, most importantly, to Scott Gediman and Ashley Mayer for facilitating park service review of my manuscript.

This work was supported by readers, editors, writers, and friends, including George Meyers, Ron Good, John Long, John Moynier, Stewart Green, Arthur Dawson, Jim Shere, Ann Peters, Rebecca Lawton, Patrice Fusillo, Claudia Avalos, JT Long, Alison Pimentel, Laura Anderson, Julianne Roth, and Bettina Hopkins.

Thanks to the wellsprings of my Yosemite experience and my eternal friends, Kelly Knappe and Karen Charland.

Thanks to editor Mike Urban for his faith, patience, and expertise. Thanks also to the team at Lyons Press for helping to polish and present these essays, and to the team at FalconGuides, which has had my back as a guidebook writer for decades.

Finally, thanks, as always, to my loving and supportive family, and most especially, to my sons, Jesse, Cruz, and Penn.

Resources and Bibliography

BOOKS

Badé, William. *The Life and Letters of John Muir.* Published online at vault.sierraclub.org.

Bingaman, John W. *Guardians of the Yosemite: A Story of the First Rangers.* Palm Desert, CA: Desert Printers Inc., 1961.

Brechin, Gary. *Imperial San Francisco: Urban Power, Earthly Ruin.* Berkeley: University of California Press, 1999.

Brower, David (ed.). *Gentle Wilderness: The Sierra Nevada.* San Francisco: Sierra Club, 1967.

Brower, Kenneth. *Hetch Hetchy: Undoing a Great American Mistake.* Berkeley, CA: Heyday Books, 2013.

———. *Yosemite* (National Geographic Park Profiles). Washington, DC: National Geographic Society, 1990.

Bunnell, Lafayette H. *The Discovery of the Yosemite and the Indian War of 1851 Which Led to That Event.* Yosemite, CA: Yosemite Association, 1991.

Carson, Rachel. *Silent Spring.* Kindle edition; originally published in 1962.

Clark, Galen. *The Big Trees of California.* Originally published in 1907.

———. *The Yosemite Valley.* Originally published in 1910.

Duncan, Dayton. *Seeds of the Future: Yosemite and the Evolution of the National Park Idea.* Yosemite, CA: Yosemite Conservancy, 2013.

Egan, Timothy. *The Big Burn: Teddy Roosevelt and the Fire that Saved America.* Boston: Mariner Books, 2009.

Fraenkel, Jeffrey (ed.). *Carleton E. Watkins: Photographs 1861–1874.* San Francisco: Bedford Arts (in association with Fraenkel Gallery), 1989.

Ghigliere, Michael P., and Charles R. "Butch" Farabee Jr. *Off the Wall: Death in Yosemite.* Flagstaff, AZ: Puma Press, 2007.

Glazner, Allen, and Greg Stock. *Geology Underfoot in Yosemite National Park.* Missoula, MT: Mountain Press Publishing, 2010.

Greene, Linda W. *Yosemite: The Park and Its Resources* (1987), www.yosemite.ca.us/library/yosemite_resources/recent_years.html#page_778.

Hill, Lynn. *Climbing Free: My Life in the Vertical World.* New York: W. W. Norton & Company, 2005.

Johnson, Shelton. *Gloryland.* Berkeley, CA: Counterpoint Press, 2009.

Johnston, Hank. *Guide to the Yosemite Cemetery.* Yosemite, CA: Yosemite Association, 1997.

———. *Railroads of the Yosemite Valley.* Long Beach, CA: Johnston-Howe Publications, 1963.

———. *The Yosemite Grant 1864–1906: A Pictorial History.* Yosemite, CA: Yosemite Association, 2008.

———. *Yosemite's Yesterdays.* Yosemite, CA: Flying Spur Press, 1989.

King, Clarence. *Mountaineering in the Sierra.* Lincoln: University of Nebraska Press, 1997. Originally published in 1872 by J. R. Osgood & Co.

Kroeber, Theodora. *Ishi in Two Worlds.* Berkeley: University of California Press, 1961.

LaPena, Frank, Craig D. Bates, and Steven P. Medley. *Legends of the Yosemite Miwok.* Berkeley, CA: Yosemite Association and Heyday Books, 1981, 1993, 2007.

Meyers, George. *Yosemite Climbs.* Denver, CO: Chockstone Press, 1982.

Meyers, George, and Don Reid. *Yosemite Climbs.* Denver, CO: Chockstone Press, 1987.

Muir, John. *The Mountains of California.* New York: Penguin Classics edition, 1997. Originally published in 1894.

———. *My First Summer in the Sierra.* Boston: Houghton Mifflin Co., 1911.

———. *The Story of My Boyhood and Youth.* Madison: University of Wisconsin Press, 1964. Originally published in 1913.

———. *The Wild Muir.* Yosemite, CA: Yosemite Association, 1994.

———. *The Yosemite.* New York: Random House Modern Library Classic edition, 2003. Originally published in 1912.

Olmsted, Frederick L. *Yosemite and the Mariposa Grove: A Preliminary Report.* Yosemite, CA: Yosemite Association, 2009. Originally published in 1865.

Radanovich, Leroy. *Images of America: Yosemite Valley.* Mount Pleasant, CA: Arcadia Publishing, 2004.

———. *Yosemite National Park and Vicinity.* Mount Pleasant, CA: Arcadia Publishing, 2006.

Roney, Bob. *The Road Guide to Yosemite.* San Francisco: Yosemite Conservancy, 2013.

Roper, Steve. *A Climber's Guide to Yosemite Valley.* San Francisco: Sierra Club, 1971.

Ross, Michael Elsohn. *Nature Art with Chiura Obata.* Minneapolis, MN: Carolrhoda Books Inc., 2000.

Runte, Alfred. *Yosemite: The Embattled Wilderness.* Lincoln: University of Nebraska Press, 1990.

Russell, Carl P. *One Hundred Years in Yosemite,* Omnibus Edition. Yosemite, CA: Yosemite Association, 1992.

Salcedo-Chourré, Tracy. *Hiking Waterfalls in Northern California.* Guilford, CT: Globe Pequot/FalconGuides (an imprint of Rowman & Littlefield), 2015.

Sargent, Shirley. *Galen Clark, Yosemite Guardian.* Yosemite, CA: Flying Spur Press, 1981.

———. *Pioneers in Petticoats.* Yosemite, CA: Flying Spur Press, 1998.

———. *Wawona's Yesterdays.* Yosemite, CA: Yosemite Association, 1978. Online at www .yosemite.ca.us/library/wawonas_yesterdays.

———. *Yosemite: The First 100 Years.* Yosemite, CA: Yosemite Park & Curry Co., 1988.

Shirley, James C. *The Redwoods of Coast and Sierra.* Berkeley: University of California Press, 1940. Online at www.nps.gov/parkhistory/online_books/shirley/index.htm.

Simpson, John W. *Dam! Water, Power, Politics, and Preservation in Hetch Hetchy and Yosemite National Park.* New York: Pantheon Books, 2005.

Stillman, Andrea G. *Yosemite: Ansel Adams.* Boston: Little, Brown and Co., 2014.

Trexler, Keith. *The Tioga Road: A History 1883–1961.* Yosemite, CA: Yosemite Natural History Association, 1961. www.yosemite.ca.us/library/tioga_road.

Van Ommeren, Alice. *Yosemite's Historic Hotels and Camps.* Mount Pleasant, CA: Arcadia Publishing, 2013.

Whitney, Josiah D. *The Yosemite Guide-Book.* Originally published in 1869. Chapter 3: The Yosemite Valley, www.yosemite.ca.us/library/the_yosemite_book/chapter_3.html.

Wuerthner, George (ed.) *Wild Fire: A Century of Failed Forest Policy.* Sausalito, CA: Island Press, 2006.

ARTICLES, STUDIES, AND REPORTS

Bingaman, John W. *The Ahwahneechees: A Story of the Yosemite Indian* (1966), published on yosemite.ca.us.

———. *Pathways: A Story of Trails and Men* (1968), reprinted at www.yosemite.ca.us.

Breck, Stewart W., Nathan Lance, and Victoria Seher. "Selective Foraging for Anthropogenic Resources by Black Bears: Minivans in Yosemite National Park." US Department of Agriculture Wildlife Service and Yosemite National Park, 2009.

Brockman, C. Frank. "Development of Transportation to Yosemite," *Yosemite Nature Notes* (1943), www.yosemite.ca.us/library/yosemite_nature_notes/22/22-6.pdf.

"Celebrating George Wright: A Retrospective on the 20th Anniversary of the GWS," George Melendez Wright 1904–1936: A Voice on the Wing. www.georgewright.org/174emorylloyd.pdf.

"The Civilian Conservation Corps (CCC) in Yosemite," *Yosemite,* Yosemite Association journal (Fall 2005).

Clark, Galen. *Indians of the Yosemite Valley and Vicinity: Their History, Customs and Traditions.* San Francisco: H. S. Crocker & Co., 1904. Reprinted on yosemite.ca.us.

Crampton, C. Gregory. "The Discovery of Yosemite and the Mariposa Indian War 1850–1851: The Diaries of Robert Eccleston," *Yosemite Nature Notes* (1958).

Ernst, Emil F. "The Floods of Yosemite Valley," *Yosemite Nature Notes* (March 1952), www.yosemite.ca.us/library/yosemite_nature_notes/31/31-3.pdf.

"The Giant Sequoia," from the *Handbook of Yosemite National Park* by Willis Linn Jepson (professor of botany at University of California, Berkeley), 1921. Reprinted at www.yosemite.ca.us/library/handbook_of_yosemite_national_park/sequoia.html.

Gibbons, Robert P., and Harold F. Heady. "Influence of Modern Man on the Vegetation of Yosemite Valley." University of California Division of Agricultural Sciences, Yosemite Natural History Association, 1964.

Graber, Daniel, and Marshall White. *Management of Black Bears and Humans in Yosemite National Park.* Department of Forestry and Conservation, UC Berkeley.

Hopkins III, John B., and Steven T. Kalinowski. *The Fate of Transported American Black Bears in Yosemite National Park.* University of California, Santa Cruz, and Montana State University, 2013.

Hubbard, Douglass. "Ghost Mines of Yosemite" (1958). www.yosemite.ca.us/library/ghost_mines/discovery.html.

Jamison, Michael. "The Great Fire of 1910," *Montana Outdoors* magazine, Montana Fish, Wildlife & Parks, 2012.

Kroeber, A. L. *Indians of Yosemite (Handbook of Yosemite National Park)*. Berkeley: University of California, 1921.

Leonard, Zenas. *Adventures of a Mountain Man: The Narrative of Zenas Leonard*. New York: R. R. Donnelley, 1934.

Meral, Gerald H. "Beyond and Beneath O'Shaughnessy Dam: Options to Restore Hetch Hetchy Valley and Replace Water and Energy Supplies," Restore Hetch Hetchy, 2005.

Muir, John. "The Hetch Hetchy Valley," *Sierra Club Bulletin*, Vol. VI, No. 4 (1908), http://vault.sierraclub.org/ca/hetchhetchy/hetch_hetchy_muir_scb_1908.html.

Parker, Harry C. *Mammals of Yosemite National Park*, 1952, www.yosemite.ca.us/library/mammals_of_yosemite/hoofed_mammals.html.

Parker, Julia. *Q&A with a Yosemite Insider: Julia Parker*. Yosemite Conservancy, 2013, www.yosemiteconservancy.org/sites/default/files/useruploads/JP-extended%20article%20final.pdf.

"Petition of Marsden Manson, City Engineer of San Francisco, on Behalf of the City and County of San Francisco, to the Secretary of the Interior Department, to Reopen the Matter of the Application of James D. Phelan for Reservoir Rights of Way in the Hetch Hetchy Valley and Lake Eleanor Sites in the Yosemite National Park." Online at www.sfmuseum.org/hetch/hetchy2.html.

"The Story of Lost Arrow," posted by John Long on Facebook, February 2015.

Taylor, Mrs. H. J. *The Last Survivor*. Reprinted by permission of the Regents of the University of California. San Francisco: Johnck and Seeger, 1932.

Taylor, Katherine Ames. "Return of the Mariposa Battalion," *Yosemite Tales and Trails*, 1934. Reprinted on www.yosemite.ca.us.

Trexler, Keith A. *The Tioga Road: A History 1883–1961*. Yosemite, CA: Yosemite Natural History Association, 1961, 1980.

"Unusual July 10, 1996, Rock Fall at Happy Isles, Yosemite National Park, California," *Geological Society of America Bulletin* (January 2000), landslides.usgs.gov/docs/wieczorek/happyisles.pdf.

"The Wawona Hotel and Thomas Hill Studio," from *Architecture in the Parks: A National Historic Landmark Theme Study*. www.nps.gov/parkhistory/online_books/harrison/harrison1.htm.

"Wildlife Management in National Parks (The Leopold Report)." National Park Service, 1963. www.nps.gov/parkhistory/online_books/leopold/leopold8.htm#1.

Yosemite Conservancy (Spring/Summer 2015).

Yosemite Conservancy (Autumn/Winter 2015).

Yosemite National Park. *Cultural Landscape Report: Camp Curry Historic District, 2010*. www.nps.gov/parkhistory/online_books/yose/camp_curry_clr.pdf.

———. *Geologic Resources Inventory Report, 2012*. www.nature.nps.gov/geology/inventory/publications/reports/yose_gri_rpt_view.pdf.

"The Yosemite Rock Fall of July 10, 1996" (Seismo Blog), University of California Berkeley Seismological Report, seismo.berkeley.edu/blog/seismoblog.php/1996/12/10/199.
"Yosemite Valley National Historic District Nomination Form," www.nps.gov/yose/learn/historyculture/upload/Yosemite-Valley-Historic-District.pdf.

FILMS

The National Parks: America's Best Idea. Ken Burns and Dayton Duncan (six-episode series, PBS, 2009).
Secret Yosemite. A National Geographic film, 2007.
Valley Uprising: Yosemite's Rock Climbing Revolution. Sender Films, 2014.
Yosemite Nature Notes 4: Half Dome (video), www.nps.gov/yose/learn/photosmultimedia/ynn4-halfdome.htm.

WEBSITES

General
geonames.usgs.gov
hathitrust.org
lib.berkeley.edu/libraries/bancroft-library/digital-collections
nps.gov
    n94044.eos-intl.net/N94044/OPAC/Search/SimpleSearch.aspx
    nps.gov/media/multimedia-search.htm?q=Yosemite
    nps.gov.yose
sierraclub.org
    vault.sierraclub.org
yosemite.ca.us
    yosemite.ca.us/library/yosemite_nature_notes

Historic Photos
nps.gov/hfc/cfm/npsphoto2.cfm
nps.gov/media/photo/gallery.htm
nps.gov/museum/centennial/treasures/yose.htm

The Ahwahneechee
courts.ca.gov/3066.htm
linguistics.berkeley.edu/~survey/languages/california-languages.php
sacred-texts.com

The Mariposa Battalion
vault.sierraclub.org/history/bulletin/#R
yosemite.ca.us/library/indians_of_the_yosemite/chapter_1.html
yosemite.ca.us/library/yosemite_indians_and_other_sketches/indians.html

The Cutting Edge

climbing.com/climber/10-things-you-didnt-know-about-yosar
irma.nps.gov/Stats/SSRSReports/Park%20Specific%20Reports/Annual%20Park
     %20Recreation%20Visitation%20(1904%20-%20Last%20Calendar%20
     Year)?Park=YOSE
nps.gov/featurecontent/yose/anniversary/about
nps.gov/featurecontent/yose/anniversary/timeline/in-1864
nps.gov/media/video/view.htm?id=E716F219-C864-EBCC-6A4A60D9DEF0C715
nps.gov/parkhistory/hisnps/NPSHistory/timeline_annotated.htm
nps.gov/yose/learn/historyculture/buffalo-soldiers.htm
nps.gov/yose/learn/management/enabling_leg.htm
150.parks.ca.gov/?page_id=27592
sierracollege.edu/ejournals/jsnhb/v5n1/conness.html
yosemite.ca.us/library/yosemite_resources/state_grant.html#page_51
yosemiteconservancy.org/history
yosemitevalleyrailroad.com/LOGGING.COMPANIES/YosemiteLumber.html
yosemitevalleyrr.com/prototype/history

Building an Icon

nps.gov/parkhistory/online_books/harrison/harrison15p.htm#1
nps.gov/parkhistory/online_books/rusticarch/chap10.htm
nps.gov/yose/learn/historyculture/charlotte-ewing.htm
nps.gov/yose/learn/historyculture/hutchings.htm
nps.gov/yose/learn/historyculture/mine-site.htm
nps.gov/yose/learn/historyculture/navy-hospital.htm
nps.gov/yose/learn/historyculture/upload/Merced-Lake-High-Sierra-Camp-Historic-
     District.pdf
yosemite.ca.us/library/the_great_yo-semite_valley/1.html#page_1
yosemite.ca.us/library/yosemite_resources/images/illustration_80.jpg
yosemite.ca.us/library/yosemite/67-4.pdf

The Quiet Giants

berkeleyheritage.com/essays/wawona.html
nps.gov/parkhistory/online_books/harrison/harrison1.htm
nps.gov/parkhistory/online_books/shirley/sec10.htm
nps.gov/seki/learn/nature/upload/FINAL-30-Largest-Sequoias.pdf
nps.gov/yose/blogs/Roadside-Naturalist-Effects-of-the-Mono-Winds.htm
nps.gov/yose/learn/historyculture/galen-clark.htm vault.sierraclub.org/john_muir_
     exhibit/people/clark.aspx
sequoiaparksfoundation.org/2011/a-new-tallest-giant-sequoia
yosemite.ca.us/forum/viewtopic.php?t=1564
yosemite.ca.us/library/handbook_of_yosemite_national_park/sequoia.html
yosemite.ca.us/library/the_yosemite_book/chapter_5.html
yosemite.ca.us/mariposa_grove_of_giant_sequoias

John Muir

nytimes.com/learning/general/onthisday/bday/0421.html

vault.sierraclub.org/john_muir_exhibit/life/chronology.aspx

vault.sierraclub.org/john_muir_exhibit/life/life_and_letters/chapter_10.aspx

vault.sierraclub.org/john_muir_exhibit/life/life_and_letters/chapter_11.aspx

vault.sierraclub.org/john_muir_exhibit/people/genealogy_muir.aspx

vault.sierraclub.org/john_muir_exhibit/people/muirl.aspx

Hetch Hetchy

bawsca.org/water-supply/hetch-hetchy-water-system

d3n8a8pro7vhmx.cloudfront.net/hetchhetchy/pages/40/attachments/original/
    1410972547/Comments_on_the_Invasion_of_Yosemite_NP_(Bulletin__2__1913)
    .pdf?1410972547

hetchhetchy.org

nps.gov/grba/learn/management/organic-act-of-1916.htm

nps.gov/yose/blogs/Remember-Hetch-Hetchy-The-Raker-Act-and-the-Evolution-of
    -the-National-Park-Idea.htm

sfwater.org

vault.sierraclub.org/ca/hetchhetchy/index.asp

vault.sierraclub.org/ca/hetchhetchy/oshaugnessy_dam_1998.html

vault.sierraclub.org/ca/hetchhetchy/timeline.asp

water.ca.gov/pubs/environment/hetch_hetchy_restoration_study/hetch_hetchy_restora
    tion_study_report.pdf

Images of Yosemite

anseladams.com/ansel-adams-the-role-of-the-artist-in-the-environmental-movement

babel.hathitrust.org/cgi/pt?id=uc1.b2982597;view=1up;seq=21

berkeleyside.com/2014/12/19/chiura-obata-a-story-of-resilience-a-passion-for-yosemite

biography.com/people/eadweard-muybridge-9419513#personal-life-and-death

carletonwatkins.org

getty.edu/art/collection/artists/2046/eadweard-j-muybridge-american-born-england
    -1830-1904

jstor.org/stable/25160951?seq=1#page_scan_tab_contents

nps.gov/yose/learn/historyculture/thomas-hill.htm

undiscovered-yosemite.com/yosemite-photographers.html

vault.sierraclub.org/history/ansel-adams

vault.sierraclub.org/john_muir_exhibit/people/lyman.aspx

yosemite.ca.us/library/yosemite_indians_and_other_sketches/early_artists.html

yosemite.ca.us/library/yosemite_nature_notes/15/15-8.pdf

yosemite.ca.us/library/yosemite_nature_notes/38/38-6.pdf

yosemite.ca.us/library/yosemite_wildflower_trails

yosemiterenaissance.org/index.html

The Climbers

adventureblog.nationalgeographic.com/2015/09/15/yosemite-climber-hans-florine
    -makes-his-100th-ascent-of-the-nose
alpinist.com/doc/web15x/newswire-half-dome-rockfall
highwire.org/~galic/stanford/halfdome
highwire.stanford.edu/~galic/stanford/halfdome/john_conway.html
nasonline.org/publications/biographical-memoirs/memoir-pdfs/brewer-william-h.pdf
nytimes.com/2015/06/14/sports/dean-potter-final-yosemite-jump.html?smid=fb-share
outsideonline.com/1925166/valley-uprising
rockandice.com/lates-news/dean-potter-sets-new-half-dome-fkt
supertopo.com/climbers-forum/2652220/Who-was-John-Salath-Previously
    -Unpublished-Story-by-Allen-Steck
supertopo.com/climbing/thread.php?topic_id=68674
vault.sierraclub.org/education/leconte
washingtonpost.com/news/morning-mix/wp/2015/05/18/dean-potter-extreme-climber
    -who-risked-falling-in-order-to-fly-dies-in-base-jumping-accident

Sculpting Yosemite

earthquake.usgs.gov/earthquakes/states/events/1872_03_26.php
firefall.info
nature.nps.gov/geology/inventory/publications/reports/yose_gri_rpt_view.pdf
pnsn.org/outreach/about-earthquakes/plate-tectonics
world-of-waterfalls.com/yosemite-waterwheel-falls.html
yosemite.ca.us/library/matthes/john_muir_glacial_theory.html
yosemite.ca.us/library/the_yosemite_book/chapter_3.html; Chapter 3: The Yosemite
    Valley, from Josiah Whitney's *The Yosemite Guide-Book.*
yosemite.ca.us/library/yosemite_nature_notes/13/13-6.pdf
yosemitefirefall.com/yosemite-firefall-glacier-point

Yosemite Wildlife

bear.org/website/bear-pages/black-bear/hibernation/191-5-stages-of-activity-and
    -hibernation.html
dfg.ca.gov/wildlife/hunting/bear/population.html
jeffreytrust.wordpress.com/tag/bears
jeffreytrust.wordpress.com/2010/01/03/scaring-a-bear-away
livescience.com/43818-yosemite-bears-food-stealing-study.html
mvz.berkeley.edu/Grinnell.html
nationalparktraveler.com/review/2015/08%E2%80%8B/speaking-bears-bear-crisis-and
    -tale-rewilding-yosemite-sequoia-and-other-national
news.ucsc.edu/2014/03/yosemite-bears.html
nps.gov/parkhistory/online_books/rusticarch/chap10.htm
nps.gov/yose/blogs/Bear-Series-Part-Three-The-Return-of-the-California-Grizzly.htm
nps.gov/yose/blogs/Bear-Series-Part-Four-Bear-Men-of-the-American-Frontier.htm
nps.gov/yose/blogs/Peregrine-Falcons.htm
nps.gov/yose/learn/nature/sheep.htm

nps.gov/yose/learn/nature/upload/george-wright-fact-sheet.pdf
scpr.org/programs/take-two/2012/10/24/28981/monarch-the-sad-amazing-story-of-the
    -bear-on-calif
sfgate.com/news/article/CA-grizzly-bear-Monarch-a-symbol-of-suffering-2372855
    .php
washingtonpost.com/news/wonkblog/wp/2015/06/16/chart-the-animals-that-are-most
    -likely-to-kill-you-this-summer
yosemite.ca.us/library/yosemite/63-4.pdf

Yosemite's Furies
alpinist.com/doc/web15x/newswire-half-dome-rockfall
eosweb.larc.nasa.gov/project/misr/gallery/california_rim_fire
foresthistory.org/ASPNET/Policy/Fire/FamousFires/1910Fires.aspx
georgewright.org/1162vanwagtendonk.pdf
motherjones.com/environment/2013/08/rim-fire-yosemite-explainer
nature.nps.gov/geology/inventory/publications/reports/yose_gri_rpt_view.pdf
nps.gov/seki/learn/nature/sequoia-fire-history.htm
nps.gov/yose/learn/nature/rockfall.htm
nps.gov/yose/learn/news/ahwiyahrockfall.htm
scpr.org/news/2013/08/26/38893/rim-fire-one-of-top-10-largest-fires-in-yosemite-h
sierranevada.ca.gov/factsheets/10.31rimfirefactsheet.pdf
yosemite.ca.us/library/yosemite_nature_notes/47/47-12.pdf

Index